Losing *You* Too Soon

BERNADETTE KEAGGY

HARVEST HOUSE PUBLISHERS
Eugene, Oregon 97402

Cover by Koechel Peterson & Associates, Minneapolis, Minnesota

LOSING YOU TOO SOON

Copyright © 2002 by Bernadette Keaggy
Published by Harvest House Publishers
Eugene, Oregon 97402

Library of Congress Cataloging-in-Publication Data
Keaggy, Bernadette.
    Losing you too soon / Bernadette Keaggy.
       p. cm.
    Rev. ed. of: A deeper shade of grace. 1996.
    Includes bibliographical references.
    ISBN 0-7369-0871-4
    1. Consolation. 2. Miscarriage—Religious aspects—Christianity. 3. Infants (Premature)—Death—Religious aspects—Christianity. 4. Bereavement—Religious aspects—Christianity. 5. Keaggy, Bernadette. 6. Keaggy, Phil. I. Keaggy, Bernadette. Deeper shade of grace. II. Title.

BV4907 .K43 2002
248.8'66—dc21   2001051580

Printed in the United States of America.

  02 03 04 05 06 07 08 09 10 / VP-CF / 10 9 8 7 6 5 4 3 2 1

Contents

Foreword

Bernadette Keaggy, my wife of 28 years, is a special gift to me. She is a warmhearted, compassionate woman who has graced my life these many years as my dearest friend and the mother of my children. There was a time, however, when the two of us faced uncertainty about becoming parents, about being a mother and father of our own children. This is a true story taken from real events in our lives. It is a story, even though a fair amount of time has passed, difficult to retell.

As Bernadette poured her heart and soul into the writing of this book, I've watched her relive the hopes and dreams, the tragic disappointments and pain of our early years of marriage when she was unable to carry a child to term. This book reveals those personal struggles and this private area of our lives to help bring others *hope.*

Like other people, we have faced tragedy, but we have grown through the pain. We were able to do so because of the decision in our lives to follow the One who is Love incarnate, the One who promises us grace and hope, despite the circumstances. The problem from a human standpoint is that some of the paths we walk upon are frightening and dark. And often only through tears are we able to see God's hand of mercy and grace.

This book has already been read by many people in its previous publication. I personally have met many who asked me to thank Bernadette for her book. They tell me that it has helped them, comforted them, and nourished their faith in God's good mercy and divine providence. Many of their letters with the story of their own losses are included throughout the book.

My prayer is that this newly revised edition will help you stake your lives on this very fact: "Our times are in his hands." God sees and understands our hopes, dreams, disappointments, suffering, and pain.

Although this is not a "how-to" book with quick, easy solutions, our prayer is that it will serve to be an encouragement to you to look upward into the face of Love.

Phil Keaggy

Acknowledgments

Thanks to the people at Harvest House, including Terry Glaspey and Carolyn McCready, for believing in this book as a continual source of help for grieving parents; Cindy Crosby for graciously taking on this project with her editing skills and knowledge; Elinor Madeira and the many other people who so willingly shared their personal stories; and David Hazard for the time, energy, and editing skills he devoted to the original manuscript.

Thanks also to Phil and our children for their loving support and encouragement throughout this writing process. I love you.

Prologue

Once there was a young married couple, Phil and Bernadette. Phil was an up-and-coming Christian musician, and Bernadette was a small-town girl who had married him fresh out of high school. Their only desire was to serve the Lord, love each other, and start a family. The future looked bright.

"For I know the plans I have for you," declares the Lord, *"plans to prosper you and not to harm you, plans to give you hope and a future."*

JEREMIAH 29:11

Chapter One

The Valley of the Shadow: Stillbirth

There was something exceptional about the fall season that settled over New York that year. The trees were sprinkled across the hills in a collage of orange, scarlet, and yellow. The air was crisp and clean. I was well into my first pregnancy, and the world seemed beautiful. I went regularly for my monthly checkups, and everything was progressing smoothly. My husband, Phil, often went with me, and as we listened to the baby's heartbeat grow stronger, we were delighted. There was something sacred about the fact that a child was growing within me.

It was 1975, and we had been married almost two years. That spring I began waking up feeling queasy each morning. By the second week of feeling sick, I decided to confirm my suspicions and visit the local women's clinic in Ithaca for a pregnancy test. I saw the doctor, had a blood test, and waited for what seemed like forever for the verdict: positive.

As I drove home, I was hardly able to contain myself. I burst into our house and into Phil's arms. "We're going to have a baby!" I said.

Immediately, we called my parents, who were thrilled. Then we let our friends in on our great news. We were in good company, because many of our friends were starting families as well.

This was a tremendous new responsibility for us. Me, a mother? Phil, a father? Was it possible? It happens every day to people—but now it was happening to *us,* and it felt wonderful.

Our neighbor, Lonnie, had just found out she was pregnant too. As the weeks went by, we enjoyed sharing our new experiences with each other. We'd get together for our weekly bread baking and talk about baby names, and who our children would most resemble.We compared our expanding bellies.

The summer passed quickly, and we marked off the months. We were in awe of the whole birth process and read page by page a book on the first nine months of life. There was new meaning in Psalm 139:13: "For you created my inmost being; you knit me together in my mother's womb." God was forming this child within me, and I was deeply at peace.

One Saturday that fall, Phil and I stopped at a roadside stand to purchase some fresh apple cider. As we looked over the huge baskets of apples, I felt a flutter inside me. "Phil, quick, put your hand on my side," I said excitedly. "The baby—I felt him move!" Phil's eyes widened as he rested his hands on my stomach. It was the first "hello" from this little person who was coming to us from God.

As the weeks passed, the flutters gave way to gentle kicks. Phil would wrap his arms around me in bed at night and sing silly little songs. *"Baby, baby you're so sweet. Baby, baby, I feel your feet! Baby, baby, you're so neat!"*

This child was going to be musical, I thought, and have a great sense of humor.

As I entered my fifth month of pregnancy, my belly expanded greatly. I was glad to be young and healthy and feeling great with this child. My mother and I talked regularly on the phone, and I'd listen to her stories about when she was pregnant with me. She sent me maternity stretch panels to sew into my regular jeans, which no longer fit. And I felt God stretching my heart daily, making room for this little one.

I felt ready for the adventure ahead.

Sunday, November 1, dawned cold and crisp. Several inches of snow had fallen, not unusual for upstate New York. Bundled up, we headed for the 10 A.M. worship service. I settled myself into one of the few theater seats that were lined up against the wall. Everyone else sat cross-legged on the carpeted floor. The sun streamed in through the stained-glass windows and left lovely colored patterns throughout the roomful of praying, singing, clapping people. Phil sat on stage and helped lead the singing.

As I sang along, my mind began to wander. My tummy felt very taut. I started to feel my uterus tightening up. Again. And again. Slowly and consistently. Now I was preoccupied. What was this?

Halfway through the service, I got up and walked to the back of the room to stand against the wall. I tried to put out of mind any worried thoughts. *It's nothing. I probably didn't sleep as well as I could have last night.* I was feeling worse by the minute. I couldn't wait for the service to end. Finally, I made my way to Phil and whispered that I wasn't well. Anxious, we headed home quickly and called Dr. Nelson.

"I seem to be having some contractions that are getting uncomfortable," I told him. Dr. Nelson didn't seem worried. "You're probably experiencing some Braxton Hicks contractions. That's normal for your fifth month. Try some gentle rocking on your hands and knees. That should cause them to ease up. Call me at the office on Monday if they are still bothering you."

I hung up and tried to do the exercises he suggested. But the pains worsened.

"Phil, call Lonnie to come over, please," I said. "I've got to lie down."

When Lonnie walked into the bedroom, she looked concerned. "What's the matter?" she asked. By now I was rocking back and forth in agony, unable to answer. Then, as if someone had pulled a plug, my water broke and amniotic fluid gushed onto the bedroom floor.

Phil raced for the phone to call the doctor, and Lonnie held my hand while her husband, Stan mopped the floor. Dr. Nelson told us to rush to the hospital, where he would meet us. As we headed for Tompkins County Hospital in Ithaca, about 25 minutes away, I winced over every bump Phil tried cautiously to avoid. I had no words for what I was feeling, but my heart was sick with fear.

Oh, little baby, are you all right?

Phil held my hand and prayed out loud.

By the time we got to the hospital, my labor was in full swing. The nurses helped me out of the wheelchair and onto the gurney, then helped me change into a hospital gown. They checked the progress of my labor and found that I was fully dilated. The doctor nodded to the nurse to scrub up as they ushered me into the delivery room. I was thrashing in agony. Fear and panic overwhelmed me as they wheeled me into the cold, sterile delivery room. The large swinging doors slammed in Phil's face, leaving him on the outside in total dismay.

This is not how it's supposed to be! I thought. I was overwhelmed by everything. I hadn't even taken childbirth classes—they didn't start until the next month.

The nurse was squeezing my arm, trying to give me instructions that I was too out of it to really understand. "Mrs. Keaggy, all I can give you is a local anesthetic," she said. "The baby is small and coming quickly."

"Bear down—and push!" another nurse chimed in.

With that, I saw my firstborn son emerge—perfectly silent, unmoving. The doctor laid him on my stomach.

There was utter serenity on his tiny face.

Suddenly, more contractions came, and a second son emerged, still in his amniotic sac. Then, after several more agonizing contractions, a third son was born. Unlike the first two, this little one had an ounce of life in him.

The doctor reached for a large oxygen mask and virtually covered the baby's face as he held this tiny body in the palm of one hand. In a few minutes, the baby stopped breathing altogether.

It was over.

I looked at my three perfectly formed small sons lying on my stomach. With my hand I stroked their dark, soft hair. Every detail of their bodies was complete, right down to their eyelashes and fingernails. Their beautiful bowed lips seemed relaxed and at peace. This was my one and only moment of contact with my sons.

Tears ran down my face as my heart broke.

Suddenly, the nurse removed the babies. "The cut-off point for when you have to have a proper burial and funeral is six months. The doctor thinks these babies were about 22 weeks. Do you want us to take care of things?"

Physically and emotionally I was exhausted. Part of me was still in a fog, lost in thought, trying to make sense out of what happened. I nodded to the nurse weakly. "OK," I whispered. It didn't register exactly what they would do with the triplets, but the last time I saw my sons, the nurse was wheeling them out of the room on a gurney.

The clock said 6:15 P.M. as I was taken into recovery. It was all over in a few short hours. Phil was waiting for me, along with our pastor, Ted Sandquist. The doctor had already told Phil the news.

Phil cried as he hugged me. Ted put his arms around us and prayed quietly with words that were gentle and strong. He asked God to give us peace—to help us know that these sons were in his arms and that we would again have children.

After Ted left, Phil and I held each other. His hand traced my now-empty abdomen. We both wept. I just wanted to sleep for hours and hours.

We both had so many questions, and no answers.

Journal

Journal

Journal

For this I bless you
as the ruin falls.
The pains you give me
are more precious
than all other gains.[1]

C. S. LEWIS,
"As the Ruin Falls"

Chapter Two

How It All Began:
Phil and Bernadette's Story

All Phil and I really wanted was a good marriage based on love and honesty. We didn't want much beyond that, except a few children to share our love with—children with our eyes and characteristics and our enjoyment of life. I never thought either a good marriage or a family would be that difficult to create.

I grew up in a small town in Akron, Ohio, in the 1950s and '60s that still had small-town, middle-America simplicity. People there were mostly innocent and trusting. We never felt we had to lock our doors because we were just "safe." But mainly, I think, my security came from being raised in a home built on a solid marriage between my father and mother, who loved each other a lot. Our family made you feel like things were always going to be OK.

Slowly, I became aware of a harsher side of the world. I began to respond to fear and difficult circumstances by building walls inside myself for protection. As a teenager, I rejected my "Catholic girl" image and walked straight into "hippiedom." *Me first,* was my motto. I surrounded myself with walls, even working to keep out those I loved the most.

My friend Sharon and I would sneak off to a couple of local bars. Because Sharon was three years older, and was a friend of the family, my parents trusted us together. They would have died if they'd known I was using my sister's I.D. to get into the clubs. I was still several years underage. We didn't drink—we just went to hear the bands.

The first time we went to Oden's Den, it was dark, smoky, and loud. It was swarming with people. A group called Glass Harp was cranking out some of the hottest rock and roll I'd ever heard! Their music was incredible, and their lyrics were thoughtful.

But mostly I was attracted to the lead guitarist and singer, Phil Keaggy. He was slightly built, with a dark beard and mustache, and large, kind eyes. Even up on the stage there was something different about him— a charisma and a brightness of spirit. He didn't give off that arrogant *come-and-get-me-girls* air of a rocker.

When Glass Harp finished their set, Phil came down from the stage, dodged a guy standing next to us, and turned right into me. As if I was meant to be in *that* place at *that* time, I was eye-to-eye with him. Our eyes met, and I felt something deeper happen. He felt it too. "Hi, I'm Phil Keaggy," he said, sounding surprised. "Um...would you like a cough drop?"

That was how this talented and unassuming man was ushered into my life. Later, after the show, he invited me to a friend's house. There I met some of the nicest people I'd ever run into. No one was doing drugs. There were no couples tucked off in dark corners, hanging all over each other. Everyone was sitting in a circle, singing songs and reading from the Bible. And they were having a grand time.

I was in awe. There was something different here. These people were friendly, happy, and open. By contrast, I felt so cautious and closed. When you're trying hard to be "cool" you never let your guard down. But from the beginning, I think I knew Phil was going to open up the self-centered shell my heart was locked in.

Besides Phil's easy manner and great sense of humor, there was a certain way he talked about his spiritual beliefs—so naturally, without religious talk. He seemed to possess something that no one else had ever offered me. It was a sense of hope and promise.

"When you open your heart to God, you find out he's the only one who will never let you down," Phil would say.

Trust God? Open your heart to him? That was a totally new concept to me. From the start, Phil and I talked a lot about his faith. He made it sound real and exciting, not like religious drudgery. A whole new realm opened up to me. Phil believed in something that challenged me to reach out beyond myself, and I felt ready for the risk.

Our friendship grew quickly, and his influence was so positive I couldn't stop telling my family about him. He was so different from the shady characters I'd been going out with—and that was a welcome relief for my parents. But mostly they were amazed that I had made such a dramatic turnaround. For more than a year my relationship with them had been strained, and now I was letting them back into my private world again.

The first time Phil swung into our driveway in his little sports car—with a guitar in the passenger seat, that certain set of Dad's jaw told me what he was thinking: *Who is this older guy—a musician no less, with a sports car—and what does he want with my 15-year-old daughter?*

But as my dad and Phil chatted, I could see the walls coming down. And when Phil talked openly about the car accident only a year earlier in which his mother had been killed, Dad became all fatherly and kind. He listened with interest as Phil told him that at the funeral his older sister, Ellen, talked to him about the meaning of the gospel and how you could develop a relationship with God. Ellen told him God loved us so much, he sent his only son, Jesus, to die on the cross for us. Because he laid down the lifeblood of his only son, God himself made a way for us to come back to him.

Phil told Dad that Ellen had encouraged him to put his life in God's hands and experience the peace he'd find from trusting God the way you would trust a loving father. "When I made a decision to do that, everything changed—including my music," Phil said.

I could tell this was a relief for Dad and Mom, because they knew Phil was a "rocker." He made his faith seem simple and real.

When Phil was not on road trips with Glass Harp, we squeezed in every hour together we could find. He would drive up from his flat in Youngstown, an hour away, and we'd take long walks in the hills nearby.

Mostly, I asked questions and listened. I knew the peace and goodness Phil talked about was exactly what I wanted. Phil introduced me to the Bible. I felt I was not hearing about "religion" as I'd known it, but about a new way that lay open to me. Phil said when I trusted God and committed my life to him, God would begin to make himself real to me.

All of this spoke to me right where I was, and something inside urged me to take the risk, to take the crucial first step. Slowly, over the period of a few months, I decided to take that step.

When Glass Harp recorded their third album for Decca Records in New York City in the late spring of 1972, which fulfilled their contract, Phil decided to leave the band. He felt he could no longer live the crazy, rock-and-roll life and live out his faith at the same time. Phil wanted the freedom to play more of his own Christian music, and he wanted to play to new audiences.

Then there was *us*. Our deepening relationship was beginning to conflict with Phil's grueling schedule. Some decisions had to be made.

"Bernadette," Phil said to me, "you are my quiet place."

That was when I think I knew.

Phil's popularity was growing, and we were both caught up in the wave of young people who in the early '70s turned from hippiedom to faith in God. Phil was asked to play acoustical guitar sets at youth rallies, churches, and colleges. He was welcome to sing and speak freely about his faith.

In the fall of my senior year in high school, Phil asked my parents for permission to marry me. I knew by marrying at 18 the odds were against us. Yet I honestly felt this was part of God's design for my life and I was making the right choice. By now I had adopted the simple, open kind of faith Phil had brought into my life. I would trust God for our marriage and for my life.

On July 14, 1973, I put away my graduation robe and donned a white satin gown I had sewn myself. Mom put a garland of red roses on my head, and I happily walked down the aisle, my arm linked with Dad's. As we walked, Phil began to sing a song he wrote for me.

Your smile makes me warm inside.
Your hand in my hand, we'll walk,

and in Him we'll abide.
Happy are we.
Happy are we.[1]

There at the altar, we knew our lives were going to be as perfect as our wedding day.

That fall Phil and I began to travel from city to city with a popular group called Love Song. We became one big family with Tommy and Shelley Coomes, Jay and June Truax, Chuck and Karen Girard, and John and Linda Mehler and all their babies and toddlers. Phil and I soaked in their friendship and took mental notes on how these couples raised their children with love and discernment. *Maybe it would not be long before there would be little Keaggy children in the world too*, we thought.

When the tour ended, we halfheartedly returned to Ohio, where Phil began traveling and playing with a friend, the talented guitarist Peter York. Rather than setting a fee for concerts, they requested only enough to cover their expenses. I was amazed at how each time a bill came that we couldn't pay, a check arrived in the mail sent by someone who had been encouraged by Phil's music and wanted to help support us.

I began to learn about daily, minute-by-minute faith.

In the summer of 1974 we moved several hundred miles east of home to a Christian community called Love Inn, nestled in the rolling farmland of south-central New York state. We came to know about Love Inn through pastor Scott Ross's syndicated radio broadcast, which dealt with cutting-edge issues of Christianity. Scott played popular music and integrated into his program the new contemporary Christian music being created by musicians such as Love Song, Honeytree, and 2nd Chapter of Acts. Phil's first solo album, "What a Day," was becoming a hit, and Christian music was reaching young people in a way other methods of sharing the gospel could not. When Scott played contemporary songs, he talked about them from a spiritual standpoint, describing how they illustrated the hunger and thirst for reality and true spirituality so many young people felt. In his commentary, Scott always directed them to Jesus Christ.

As a community, we ate together, worked together, and prayed together in a barn-turned-studio-and-sanctuary. Phil and I found a small, one-story brick house about two miles from the Love Inn property, split into two apartments.

As we settled in, I found myself thriving on our simple, live-by-faith lifestyle. I didn't have a full-time job, because Phil wanted me to travel with him whenever possible. When he was out of town doing concerts and finances were tight, I helped out teaching art classes at the small community school Love Inn had started. The food on our table came mostly from Christians around the country who had heard of Love Inn and wanted to be a part of our lives. I remember thinking, *Someday we'll be on the giving end and help support people and organizations we believe in.*

After about six months, the leaders of the community urged Phil to stop traveling and doing concerts.
They felt it was important he and I build a stronger,
more stable relationship. Phil did not fully agree that
he had to stop traveling altogether to accomplish this,
but he decided to try it for a time. So he stayed home
and helped duplicate tapes of the *Scott Ross Show* that
were sent out weekly to hundreds of radio stations.
The work was laborious, but the benefits came when
we all took turns answering the thousands of letters
that flooded the mail room, each telling a unique story
of how God used the show to help someone. In doing
so we were encouraged, because God seemed to be
performing miracles in the lives of the listeners: kids
getting off drugs, marriages being salvaged.

About the time Phil was eager to do a new record
and start playing concerts again, he got a call from
Buck Herring, producer of the group 2nd Chapter of
Acts. He wanted Phil to play guitar on their new album
In the Volume of the Book. Buck also wanted to produce
a record with Phil. They agreed to work together on
Phil's second album. Phil began writing songs and
formed the Phil Keaggy Band—PKB—with four other
musicians from our area. He started touring again. I
was happy to see him working at what he knew and
loved best—his music.

We were growing as a couple, and often discussed
what it would be like to have children. We were determined to live in a way that was wide open to whatever
God had for us. We knew he loved us, and we had

vowed to show our love for him. Phil and I became each other's confidant and support. When he was pressured at work or feeling creatively stunted, we'd talk it through for hours. Then we'd hold hands and pray. Things wouldn't change immediately, but it helped to voice our thoughts and ideas and to develop patience as well. And I loved the warmth and spiritual closeness of being with this man whom I cherished.

One song Phil wrote was based on a poem by C. S. Lewis, who had become our favorite writer. The poem is called "As the Ruin Falls," and the words were intriguing to me:

All this is flashy rhetoric about loving you.
I never had a selfless thought since I was born.
I am mercenary and self-seeking through and through;
I want God, you, all friends, merely to serve my turn....[2]

Lewis seemed to be writing about spiritual discovery. Somehow he understood that even as a Christian, he still had a force inside him that worked contrary to his faith. A Christian is one who willingly submits to God's plan for his or her life. But slowly, subtly, the temptation comes to seek only what we want and to question God's goodness and wisdom. We can begin to reconstruct walls around our lives—even very spiritual-looking walls made up of all the right external behaviors, such as prayer, attending church, and Bible reading. And yet inwardly we can remain just as much in control of our lives as ever and be blind to the fact that we are no longer living as Christians, open to God, trusting God from the heart.

When Phil first sang his song for me, we discussed what Lewis must have meant. We gave God permission to do whatever it took to break down inner walls we might secretly have constructed, walls that would make our hearts hard toward him—even if it caused us great pain. Like Lewis, we wanted to be able to say, *"For this I bless you as the ruin falls. The pains you give me are more precious than all other gains."*

The true test was yet to come.

Journal

Journal

...sin, sorrow, and suffering are, and it is not for us to say that God has made a mistake allowing them. Sorrow removes a great deal of a person's shallowness, but it does not always make that person better. Suffering either gives me to myself, or it destroys me. You cannot find or receive yourself through success, because you lose your head over pride. And you cannot receive yourself through the monotony of daily life, because you give in to complaining. The only way to find yourself is in the fires of sorrow. Why it should be this way is immaterial. The fact is that it is true in the Scriptures and in human experience. You can always recognize who has been through the fires of sorrow and received himself, and you know that you can go to him in your moment of trouble and find that he has plenty of time for you. But if a person has not been through the fires of sorrow, he is apt to be contemptuous, having no respect or time for you, only turning you away.

OSWALD CHAMBERS
My Utmost for His Highest [3]

Chapter Three

Losing Again

The year that we lost the triplets, it felt like winter went on forever. When I recovered from the shock of losing our babies, I had to deal with the emotional impact of not burying our sons. Phil didn't carry this burden as much because he never saw the babies and didn't realize what fully developed human beings they were. But I knew they should have had a proper burial.

Despite the emotional pain that reared its head from time to time, Phil and I felt confident about the future. We relied on each other and believed we could get through this together. Spring proved to be busy, as Phil's first solo album was purchased for release on the newly formed record label Newsong, which was distributed by Word Records. He was scheduled to do a three-week acoustic tour with Nancy Honeytree, a female troubadour gifted with gentle words and sweet melodies. Together, they set off with a small road crew and traveled to colleges and churches throughout the

The Sobering Statistics

Each year, there are an estimated 6 million pregnancies in the United States and an estimated 1 million fetal deaths. Sixteen percent of all pregnancies end in miscarriage or stillbirth.[1] In the United States, about two-thirds of infant deaths occur in the first month after birth and are due mostly to health problems of the infant, such as birth defects, or problems during the pregnancy, such as preterm delivery.[2]

These deaths fall into one of four major categories that comprise prenatal/fetal/infant death:

- Those occurring within the first year of life from an undetermined cause—sudden infant death syndrome (SIDS)

- Those occurring during the first six months of life from some known cause—neonatal death

- stillbirth

- Those occurring during the prenatal period through miscarriage and premature birth

Some 5,000 babies fall victim to SIDS each year in the United States alone.[3] One child in every hundred births, or 33,000 babies a year, is stillborn in the United States.[4]

Midwest. I decided to join them for the second half of the tour, hoping to get my mind off what had happened. Despite the emotional pain we felt, Phil and I were confident about the future. We relied on each other and believed we could get through this together.

But babies were a sensitive topic for us, one we weren't too comfortable opening our hearts about. Oddly enough, few people—for whatever reasons— ever brought up our loss. This was unfortunate, because it kept us from realizing that we weren't the only ones going through this kind of trauma. Far from it. We weren't alone in our experience, yet at the same time, little about the subject was openly discussed. We had no one to share our pain.

Stillbirth

A baby is stillborn if it dies between the twentieth week of pregnancy and the time of birth.[5]

As for any future chance of having children, I came to my own conclusion that what happened with the triplets was an isolated incident. I was sure it would have no effect on my future pregnancies. *After all,* I thought, *it's pretty unusual to conceive triplets. If the doctor had known ahead of time I was carrying three babies, maybe things would have turned out differently.*

We recovered from the loss as best we knew how and were ready to move forward. We felt a bit like a child who falls off a bicycle—getting back on is a little scary, but to get anywhere you have to overcome your fear and keep going.

In late January, little more than three months after I left the hospital, I discovered I was pregnant again.

Phil and I wanted to believe the best for this pregnancy, but we responded differently this time around. I was somewhat reserved, and careful as I walked through the early months. I didn't discuss it much with my friends. In fact, for months I didn't tell anyone I was pregnant. I was afraid to speak the good news too loudly.

Phil, on the other hand, was quite pleased with the news and shared it openly with friends. He felt God wouldn't allow something bad to happen again. "He knows the pain we both went through," Phil told friends. "God cares for us, and this pregnancy is his way of helping us go on with our lives. He knows our hearts' desire is to have children."

Miscarriage

A miscarriage is a pregnancy loss that occurs prior to 20 weeks, before the fetus is able to survive outside its mother's womb. This tragedy occurs in about 15 percent to 20 percent of pregnancies. Most miscarriages occur in the first trimester (12 weeks) of pregnancy. Some doctors believe that as many as 50 percent of all pregnancies end in miscarriage, because some losses occur before a woman realizes she is pregnant.

—March of Dimes Web Site: www.modimes.org

Phil was a bit more cautious, though, about my physical activity. When he was around, he was quick to come to my aid in lifting anything the least bit heavy.

When I told my friend Lonnie the news, she was delighted for us. Now I felt more at ease when I'd visit her and her new baby. Yet her little girl was always a reminder of what our sons would have been doing by this time—cooing and smiling, being comforted by their mother's love.

Sometimes love hurts. And we were learning the cost of stepping out and trying again. But we were also being taught to believe the best and to trust.

Besides, now that I had felt the maternal bond between mother and child, I wanted to experience it again.

The months passed slowly. Winter turned into spring. Late one May afternoon, as I walked around Freeville, I noticed a garage sale sign and went over to check out the merchandise. Planted in the middle of the lawn was a big blue and silver baby carriage. It was larger than life and seemed to tease me, daring me to buy it.

I stood there, wavering back and forth.

It was a little too soon to take that step. *Not yet,* I thought.

I turned and walked home.

When I talked to my mom, she always cautioned me to take care of myself. Don't overdo it. Rest. Stop traveling. But physically I felt just fine.

My doctor assured me in my fifth month that
everything was normal. I felt gentle kicks almost every
day now, and I was very noticeably with child. When
Phil went out of town for concerts, he always made
sure there was someone to stay with me and I was in
good hands. I think he was afraid I would do too much
when he was gone. Sometimes my caution got the best
of me, making me leery of everything I ate, drank, or
did. I guess a small part of me wondered if I was
somehow at fault for losing the triplets.

By this time, our losses from the first pregnancy
were rarely mentioned. Sympathetic listeners were
hard to find. Friends assumed all was well, and we
were already anticipating another child. Any secret
fears Phil or I had were kept between us and seldom
even voiced to each other.

As I entered my sixth month, I breathed a small
sigh of relief and allowed myself to get excited. I was
going to be a mom!

Now I could walk through the baby department of
a store and not cringe. Phil and I started talking
seriously about names. We both loved the name *Ryan*
for a boy, though a girl's name eluded us. I signed us
up for a series of childbirth classes that would begin in
September.

Phil's work continued to go well. *Love Broke
Through*, Phil's second album, was finally recorded and
released. The demand for concerts increased. We
began to relax more about the baby and started

looking for a larger apartment, something with two bedrooms and a yard. When I was about six and one-half months along we discovered the perfect place—a huge old farmhouse that had been converted into two apartments. We rented one immediately.

Our landlords were dairy farmers who went out of their way to help us get settled. They were happy to let us repaint the living room and kitchen. Upstairs there was a large bedroom with a tiny room off of it that Phil could use for practicing his guitar or writing music. Down the hall was a medium-sized room, perfect for the baby. It had large windows that over-looked the backyard. I could already see a sandbox, and a baby swing attached to the beautiful old maple tree. The room was painted baby blue, so we decided to leave it, knowing it must be a sign of good things. Shelves lined one wall, and in my mind I pictured them filled with books and toys. A lovely wooden crib and changing table would just fit against the slanted ceilings. I reminded myself to start looking at garage sales for good used baby furniture.

We spent most of our days getting the new apart-ment ready. We were confident and happy. Everything was going to be perfect.

One morning, some friends came over to help us paint. As we laughed and talked, the fresh paint slowly transformed the old farmhouse into our home. We ended the night with four large pizzas, grateful for all our friends' help and support. By midnight, Phil and I headed back to our old apartment, tired and happy. I crawled into bed, exhausted and glad to be off my feet. Phil reached over and patted my stomach, and the baby responded with several reassuring kicks.

As I drifted off to sleep, I felt myself sinking into a deep sense of peace and security that came from believing that God was about to bless us. I was tired, but my mind was still active. I made a mental list of all that needed to be done. I twisted and turned, trying to get comfortable. My back was aching from all the cleaning. Finally, I fell asleep from sheer exhaustion.

The next morning, I awoke slowly, feeling a bit stiff from all the activity of the day before. Phil was still snoring as I maneuvered myself out of bed and shuffled into the kitchen to make some coffee. I felt a bit strange, as if the baby were shifting positions. My uterus felt hard as a rock, but there was no pain. I made myself a bowl of cereal and sat down at the kitchen table, staring at my to-do list. Only half the items were crossed off. *How am I going to move all these live plants?* I wondered. Plants were an inexpensive way of using up space in those days, and I had all shapes and sizes.

I began pulling them off the windowsills one by one and filling a huge cardboard box, trying to keep my mind off the fact that I wasn't feeling that great. As I climbed up to take down a hanging pot, my body felt as if it were tied in a large knot.

I looked down to see Phil standing in the kitchen doorway. "What are you doing standing up on that high stool?" he exclaimed. For the rest of the morning, I orchestrated the action from a sitting position as Phil did the packing. I felt tired and emotional. I was afraid to tell him—afraid to hear my own voice speak it—but my uterus was in a consistent rhythm of contractions.

"Are you all right? You don't look good" Phil said worriedly. "Why don't you go take a nap? I'll finish up in here."

Silently, I headed for the bedroom. *Maybe it'll help to lie down for a while and sleep.* I dozed off for what seemed like an hour, only to be awakened by contractions accompanied with some pain.

"Phil, I think you'd better call the doctor," I moaned.

Phil looked nervous as he tried to process what I was really saying. He ran to the phone and dialed the doctor. Five minutes later he was back.

"He said to come into the office—*immediately.*"

It was late afternoon as Phil helped me out of the car. I thought, *This can't be happening again.* The 20-minute drive had seemed like two hours. Silence hung between us. I was afraid to voice my concerns until I saw the doctor, even as a million thoughts raced through my mind. I fought to control myself as the contractions steadily increased.

Leaving Phil behind in the lobby, the nurse led me straight back to the examining room, although I could barely walk.

"You're dilating," the doctor said. "I'll call the hospital and tell them you're coming."

I don't want to go to the hospital, I thought. *I'm not ready.*

During the agonizing drive, Phil broke the silence. "This can't happen a second time, can it, honey?" I stared into his questioning, pain-filled eyes, and I couldn't give him the affirmation he wanted.

As the nurses settled me into my hospital room, Phil left to call some friends to tell them what was happening. I was hooked up to an alcohol IV, which would slow down, and hopefully stop, the contractions, Dr. Bradford told me.

I was at their mercy. I had to believe they knew what they were doing. I was willing to do anything to save this baby.

I endured 24 hours of living hell as the medication took effect on my body. Phil sat by my bedside— praying, reading, sleeping. I went through phases of laughing, crying, and dozing, becoming incoherent as the medication consumed me. Then I became violently ill, reminding me of the one and only time as a teenager when I drank a whole bottle of Boone's Farm wine on a dare.

Through waves of wild pain, I wondered how this was affecting my baby. On and off, I fell into a restless sleep, only to be awakened by terrible, painful contractions.

A whole day passed.

Occasionally, Dr. Bradford came in and checked on me. I could barely hear him as he asked Phil to follow the nurse out of the room. The doctor then told the nurse to remove the IV and to prepare me for delivery.

Phil stopped by my bed and squeezed my hand. "This time I'll be with you," he whispered.

I was so doped up the labor seemed like a nightmare. A short time later, Ryan entered our world, blue and gasping for breath. He was silent in the strangely quiet delivery room. I caught only a glimpse of him as the doctor checked his vital signs. I could see the concern in the doctor's eyes as they quickly transferred Ryan to a heated incubator.

I gave birth to a preemie, born at 25 weeks' gestation, who stayed in intensive care for 217 days and struggled every day to survive, then lost her sight. The final blow was when my husband, and her father, left us. Sarah is now 18 years old, beautiful, and full of God's goodness. Throughout all my personal losses and expectations—which brought me back to the foot of the cross—I gained the greatest gift one can gain: the gift of faith. No matter what comes into my path, I know we will and can endure in his deepest grace.

JOYCE MAINLAND
No city given

"That's our son," Phil whispered in awe. "He's got to make it. He's a month further along than the triplets." Ryan weighed two and one-half pounds.

The doctor looked at us both and said softly, "There's a fifty-fifty chance, so try not to get your hopes up."

Phil and I looked at each other. "Hope? What else is there?" Phil said.

Settled back in my hospital room with Phil at my side, I waited anxiously until the doctor came in. "We'd like to take the baby to the Perinatal Center in Syracuse, about an hour away," he said. "We don't have the equipment we need here to keep him going." Phil and I agreed at once.

Before they took Ryan away in the ambulance for the hour-long ride to Syracuse, a nurse brought him into my room. "I thought you might like to see him again," she said softly. By this time he was pink, and he looked beautiful.

I reached into the incubator and gently touched my son. I carefully stroked his dark hair. He looked so fragile as I traced his beautiful little ears with my fingers. I couldn't ignore how his chest moved violently with each breath. Wide-eyed, he looked at me as if to say, "I'm trying—for you, Mom."

Phil gently squeezed my arm and said, "It's time for him to go."

I watched helplessly as Phil and Ryan disappeared through the doorway. Phil would follow the ambulance to Syracuse.

A nurse came in and tried to be cheerful. "Ready for some rest?" she asked. I was definitely ready to sleep, to shut down my emotions for a few hours. I was too tired to think about what was ahead. I drifted off....

What seemed like only minutes later was really hours. A baby's cry broke the quietness and jolted me awake. I turned my head to see a teenage girl in the bed next to me, watching her newborn crying. She made no attempt to pick him up, although he obviously wanted to be held.

"I don't want to feed him, Mama," she said. "You do it."

I watched in amazement as the older woman at her bedside picked up the baby and gave it a bottle. The baby's mother watched television and chewed gum, looking as if she'd rather be anywhere but here.

God, I don't understand, I prayed. *This young girl doesn't even want to cuddle her baby. She looks more inconvenienced than anything.*

Our son, whom I was aching to hold, was far away, fighting for his life. Things were becoming more bewildering by the minute. My prayers came out as questions. *Why God? Why this time again? Why me?*

The next morning, when my roommate was released from the hospital, I was relieved. Shortly after breakfast, Phil came in. He'd been in constant contact with the hospital about Ryan's condition. It was still a fifty-fifty chance that he'd pull through. His lungs were underdeveloped, but all two and one-half pounds of him struggled to survive.

Phil sat down on my bed and hugged and kissed me. "We've got to believe for the best. God can pull Ryan through this," he said.

I wouldn't allow myself to be too optimistic. I wanted to guard my heart—but then, where did trust come in? I *wanted* to believe Ryan would pull through, but I knew it would be a long road if he did. How many times had I heard, "All things are possible to those who believe"?

I knew my faith was being tested.

Phil sat on the corner of the bed, trying to encourage me. "All our friends are really pulling for us," he said. He looked weary, but I knew he wanted to drive up to Syracuse to see Ryan.

"Go ahead, honey, I'll be OK," I said. "I need sleep today, anyway. Go see your son."

Phil kissed me and left. The rest of the day I slept, dozing fitfully as the nurses moved in and out. I tried to pray, but my thoughts were distracted by the sound of hungry babies being taken to their mothers for feeding. I felt left out, especially since the doctor never called to give me an update on our son. Maybe in a few days I would feel well enough to go see Ryan too.

That evening a friend stopped by to visit me at the hospital. "We believe that God's going to bring Ryan through," she said confidently. "Phil sounded encouraged when he came by today."

"I hope so," I replied. "It's difficult not being there to see him. I'm sick of this place. I can't wait to leave."

She continued talking, asking me whether I had faith to believe that God could help Ryan. Suddenly, I wanted her to leave. I knew she was kind to come, but her comments seemed so flippant. This was not her problem. It wasn't going to affect *her* life if Ryan lived or died. She already had a child, and I knew she couldn't relate to me.

I yawned and felt my eyelids getting heavy. She got the message—time to go. I lay back, feeling agitated. Again I fell into a restless sleep.

The next day, Phil called me early. He was going to see Ryan first, then he'd come by and give me a report on his condition.

By early afternoon, I was anxious to know what was going on. Phil entered the room smiling. "I touched him, honey," he said. "He grabbed hold of my finger and squeezed it." Phil's eyes flashed with hope.

I managed a smile. I felt a little jealous, and I was aching to hold the baby.

We sat and chatted together, mostly about the apartment and nothing of consequence. We hadn't moved all our things yet, but Phil was working on it with some friends. I felt helpless.

"I've got a dinner invitation from Lyn and Kathy Nichols, so I'm going to leave now," Phil said at last. "I'll come by in the morning. I love you."

The nurse arrived with a tray of "gourmet cuisine." I picked at it, then pushed it aside. My thoughts were racing in a million directions. *What's really going on* with my son? What if Phil's not telling me everything? The doctor said I could leave the hospital tomorrow.

I felt out of touch with everything and everybody.

It was less than an hour later that Phil cautiously came back to my room. I was surprised to see him

---

*M*y wife, Sandy, and I have had four miscarriages. It saddens me to know I will not get to hold these children in my arms and rock them to sleep. I will not get to see them discover that the most entertaining way to eat green beans is to throw them to the dog. I will not be able to provide comfort for a scraped knee. I will not have the discussion about what is and what is not adequate time spent practicing one's piano lesson. What is comforting is the knowledge that someday, if I've lived my life according to God's will, I will be introduced to four children in Heaven above who I have loved but not known, and they will say to me, "Thank you, Dad, for giving us life." That day will more than make up for any lost time here on earth. Sandy and I have three beautiful daughters, and each one of my seven children mean as much to me as the next.

Steve McManus
Lincoln, Nebraska

again. Then I saw his eyes. He couldn't speak it, but I knew what he was going to say.

"No, not my baby!" I shouted.

Phil held me tightly and confirmed my worst fears. Ryan had died less than an hour before. He had developed hyaline membrane disease, and his lungs had ceased to function.

"My son, my son," I sobbed. "I love you. I'll always be your mother. It's not fair. This can't be happening again. *I want my baby!*"

Phil and I held each other and wept. Then the nurse came in and gave me a sedative to drown out the pain. But how could it?

Monday morning, while I prepared to leave the hospital, Phil talked with the funeral director. The small service at the chapel in the local cemetery was set for Wednesday evening.

I couldn't bear to call my mom and dad again and left it to Phil. I felt as if I was in a deep fog, looking for the door that led out to warmth and shelter. God seemed far away. I couldn't even pray, as my anger and rage got the best of me.

Phil arranged for us to stay with our friends Eric and Donna Neilson for a few days until the house was organized. When he drove me home to our new apartment to pick up a few things, we were greeted— carefully—by two dear friends, Glorya Clark and Linda Christenson. "We're still moving your things in, so everything's not quite in order," Linda said apologetically.

I sank down into a chair at the bottom of the stairs while my two friends packed what I needed for the week. I looked around the apartment that we'd been so excitedly preparing for our "family." Normally, I would have been anxious about someone else setting up my entire house, putting things away where they thought they should go, but now I didn't care. In fact, it didn't matter if I ever came back there at all.

"Will you need these?" Glorya gently repeated. Her voice brought me back to reality. I nodded silently. When I looked into my friends' eyes, I could tell they ached for us. They knew how we'd anticipated this baby.

World, go on without me—I'm checking out.

Sleep seemed to repair my shattered emotions, and I slept as much as possible. Later, I understood that this sleep was a gift from God. I didn't want to touch with a waking mind the painful thoughts that tormented me.

When Wednesday evening arrived, I put on a long burgundy flowered dress that I'd worn when I was pregnant. This time, though, I placed the belt back around my shrunken midriff and pulled it tight.

The rain was a cold mist as we headed for the funeral chapel. I knew in my heart that I was not prepared for this.

A handful of our closest friends were already there waiting quietly for us—Ted and Dawn Sandquist, Lonnie and Stan Harrington, Stuart and Linda

Ways to Honor and Remember Your Lost Baby

1. Have a memorial service or funeral service for your baby. It may be as simple as a gathering of friends, or it may be a formal service at your church or funeral home.

2. Plant a tree in your yard and watch it grow. I did this in remembrance of my dear brother, Don, who took his life. I think of him daily when I look out my window. If you live in an apartment or condo, some churches and hospitals have memorial gardens where you may plant something in memory of your child.

3. On the birthday of your child have a short family time of sharing, and lift your sorrows and cares up to God.

4. Organizations such as M.E.N.D. have a campaign, "Light a candle for our Angel Babies," and several states have issued proclamations and have Pregnancy and Infant Loss Remembrance Day as an annual event. Contact M.E.N.D. (see resource section in the back of the book) to see how you can become a part of this.

5. There are many on-line memorials where you can post a memory of your child (for example, you may create a free virtual remembrance page for your baby at www.aplacetoremember.com).

6. If you have a photo of your child, frame it and place it with other family photos.

7. Consider keeping a special journal dedicated to writing your thoughts and feelings about your child through the years. You may also use the journal pages in this book.

Scadron-Wattles, Scott and Nedra Ross, Bill and
Glorya Clark, Lyn and Kathy Nichols, Chris and Linda
Christianson, and Eric and Donna Neilson. They all
stood like statues waiting for us to make the first
move. A few hugs were exchanged.

My eyes took in the faintly lit stone chapel. It was
so cold. We were led to the small casket on a table. Two
candlesticks dimly burned on each side. I could hardly
bear to look at it. Could my son's small, frail body
really be in there?

Our close friend Scott read a few words from the
Psalms and spoke briefly. But I shut off his words. In
the tense, quiet atmosphere, I could feel the pulse in
my neck. Phil squeezed my hand so tightly the blood
rushed out of it, making me feel flushed all over. That
was all I could feel.

My mind refused to connect with my heart. I
would not let any of this touch me. I still couldn't
believe this was happening to us.

When we sang a few of Ted's worship songs, I
made a meager attempt to join in, mouthing the
words. But my mind and heart were far away. I fought
to hold back my tears for fear I couldn't stop them
once they started.

Our dear friend Bill read aloud a poem that he'd
written about Ryan. Later, we inscribed his words on
Ryan's tombstone.

Waiting for this son,
we've yearned, we've learned he's with Someone

…with Someone.

With the Lord, that's what it meant, of course.

But why? Why not with *me?* I wanted my son. I wanted all of my sons.

I didn't cry for Ryan. I knew he was safe and in no pain. He would bypass many of life's struggles—but we would miss the joy of helping him through them.

As everyone left the chapel, Phil and I stood alone for a few last moments with Ryan.

Peace to you, my son, I thought. At my side, Phil was doing his best to be strong for me, but I knew his heart was turned inside out. This was his fourth son, a son he knew only a few days. Gone were the dreams of singing him to sleep at night, of teaching him his first words. Would he have grown up to look like his papa or carried on his legacy of music? We would never know.

We left arm in arm, carrying all our questions with us. And all our tears.

After the funeral, we gathered at the Neilsons' home. When Phil and I walked in, I joined several women who were in the kitchen preparing food. As they worked, they laughed and caught up on news. As my lips quivered, I went through the motions of conversation. I tried to act as if everything was okay.

My stomach was in a sickening knot. Donna asked me what I'd like to drink, but I could hardly hear her. Her voice seemed far away. I could feel perspiration trickling down my back. My legs felt like they were going to buckle underneath me, and I collapsed into a chair.

Then the room began closing in on me. *I don't want to be here with all of these people.* My chest felt tight as I tried to take a couple of deep breaths. I could hear talking and laughing in the background as I looked desperately for a way to escape.

I was starting to panic. *I can't handle this. Where's Phil?* I scanned the room and saw him talking with Ted.

I headed for the bathroom and locked the door behind me. Leaning against the wall, I slowly sank to the floor and sobbed. I had kept up a good front long enough. Now I didn't care.

God, where are you? I'm in pain. My heart is breaking.

I wanted to scream and let my emotions out, but I was afraid nobody would understand. I didn't want my good friends to know I wasn't handling this well—that I had lost perspective and wasn't in control any longer.

I would have stayed in the bathroom until the last person left, but Donna kept knocking on the door to check on me.

"Are you OK?" she asked.

"Yes, I'm fine," I lied.

Then I heard Phil's voice at the door, and I let him in.

"I'm so sorry this happened, honey," he said. His eyes welled up with tears, and he wrapped his arms around me and tried to give me whatever small measure of comfort he had left.

When we came out, he led me straight to the bedroom. Then he went back out to thank everyone and say good-bye.

I crawled into bed and stared at the colored quilts that hung on the walls—red, yellow, bright calico. My heart was gray and dead. Despair filled the vacuum in my heart, along with anger and indifference. Everyone else was going home to their families and getting on with their lives. Where was our life headed?

Phil came into the room and curled up on the bed with me. "I don't know why this happened," he said. "Someday we'll know the answers to all our questions."

So you say, I thought.

The idealism with which we approached life was losing its shape. If God heard our prayers, then why didn't he always answer them? Putting ourselves in God's hands meant he would keep us safe, that nothing could go wrong.

But it had all gone wrong.

Was there somehow a purpose behind all this pain? I struggled, not knowing what to believe. I'd given God my life…my heart. Why was he intent on crushing it?

Journal

Journal

Journal

Growing Up in Heaven

by Nancy Honeytree Miller
Dedicated to John William Fanning and John Richard Miller VII

What if I watered the apple tree
So much that it grew all the way to Jesus
You could climb up and take a look around
and your brother could climb down to see us

You've got a brother
He was gathered in the shepherd's arms
and carried to heaven
The day he arrived
Dad and I have two sons
One in heaven and on earth
How happy we are to know
You both are alive

You're growing up in Indiana
All your friends are in apple trees
you've got a scrape and you yelled for me
He's growing up in heaven
That's the perfect place to be a boy
There's no danger there to spoil your joy

One day we'll be greeted by a handsome lad
So glad, he'll come running to see us
To show us the things he's already learned
Growing up in heaven
Adventured forever
Someday we'll be together
Growing up in Heaven [6]

Chapter Four

Dashed Hopes: Miscarriage

Life went on. After Ryan's death, Phil and I did our best to put our lives back in order. He traveled with his band doing concerts and worked on songs for a new album when he was home. The band members—Lynn Nichols, Terry Anderson, Don Cunningham, and Phil Madeira—rallied around him and gave Phil much-needed love and support, particularly when he was on the road.

Being able to express himself emotionally through his music was healing for Phil. He had put "Ryan's Song" to music, and whenever he played it in concert, inevitably he'd meet others who had lost children. He was beginning to see how God was using our experiences to help others realize they weren't alone.

His idealistic "peace-love-joy" view of Christianity began to change shape. Phil groped to hold onto the comfortable old way of thinking—looking for assurances that if we prayed and believed, things would always turn out right. That old way of thinking was failing fast.

As we grieved the loss of our babies, one of the questions that haunted me was whether there was something physically wrong with me that kept me from carrying a child to term. I sought out a doctor who dealt with difficult pregnancies such as mine. I determined that I would have some tests run before I tried to get pregnant again.

I found Dr. Harris, who specialized in high-risk pregnancies at the Perinatal Center in Syracuse, where Ryan had been hospitalized. He was knowledgeable and understanding, and he studied my health history while I filled in the details for him. Over the course of several weeks, he scheduled all sorts of tests, trying to rule out things such as a misshapen uterus, hormone problems, or blocked fallopian tubes. I felt I was on a quest, determined to find out anything that might have caused my premature labors, so I was willing to withstand all the pricks, probes, and highly uncomfortable tests to find out.

When the results were in, I anxiously made an appointment to talk with Dr. Harris.

"We've learned that several things are affecting your ability to remain pregnant," he said, "but I believe we can remedy these. Your progesterone level should remain high until you're ready to deliver. Yours is dropping down in your fifth and sixth months. We can give you hormone shots from about four months onward, on a weekly basis, to keep this level stable." I listened intently.

"You also have what is known as an incompetent cervix," he said. I had never heard of such a thing, but Dr. Harris went on to explain, "Your cervix is weak. Once the baby starts gaining considerable weight, your cervix starts dilating and proceeds into premature labor. Unfortunately, doctors can't really diagnose this until they spot a pattern of consistent premature labor, as in your case. We can remedy this problem by a delicate procedure in your fourth month of pregnancy. It's relatively simple, like having a purse-string pulled tightly around the cervix to keep it secure."

Surgery, I thought. *Now I'm getting nervous.*

"This only requires an overnight hospital stay," the doctor said.

When I was ten weeks along, my doctor sent me for an ultrasound. My husband and I were so excited knowing we would see our baby that day. The doctor doing the ultrasound was very quiet and continued to look at the screen. After several minutes she said, "I can't locate the baby. It appears this pregnancy was lost several weeks ago." My husband and I both fell apart.

SHARI DIXON
Sewickley, Pennsylvania

"Am I awake for this procedure?" I asked.

"Yes," the doctor answered, "but you're given a spinal block, or epidural, to deaden the pain. This surgery is not entirely without risk, however." I shifted around, trying to keep calm. "There is a chance that the procedure itself could cause you to miscarry. You have to weigh those risks."

I thanked him and told him I would let him know if and when I got pregnant again.

I drove back home, thinking over the things Dr. Harris proposed. Now I felt I had a tangible solution, that I'd accomplished what I set out to do. I was anxious to tell Phil when he returned from his concert dates. This doctor seemed to have a solution for my problem. It made sense to me. I was happy to have an option again—a sense of hope. But something inside of me asked, *"Is this what your hope is based on, Bernadette? On whether or not you can have children?"*

A few months later, in January 1977, I found myself pregnant for the third time. I immediately contacted Dr. Harris in Syracuse and made an appointment to see him. Phil and I went together to his office and discussed the proceedings. We had a game plan, and we were excited once again.

As the weeks passed, my old fears resurfaced, but I tried to keep them at bay with our newfound information. I wanted to be in control of the ride this time. I wanted to be a part of making this happen.

The doctor reassured me during my checkups, and confirmed the date he would perform the procedure in my fourth month. I was cautious and careful, trying not to overdo in any way.

Phil and I felt close again. We'd often take long drives along the Finger Lakes. All the grapevines were barren and dead-looking—it was difficult to believe spring would bring them back to life. "Phil," I said, "there's life within me again. It really could be different this time."

Phil squeezed my hand in response. "The older we get, the frailer life seems to be. It's not so cut-and-dried any more—not so easy to take things for granted."

We stopped at one of our favorite views along the lake. You could see slight trickles of water through the frozen ice. Huge trees hung over the lake, looking spectacular in their coating of silver ice. We were both silent, pondering God's magnificent handiwork. There was something harsh and cold here, but beautiful too—God's presence was in the midst of it all.

In late April, almost four months into my third pregnancy, I awoke one morning with mild cramping. Keenly aware of anything out of the ordinary, I decided to call my doctor.

"Dr. Harris is out of town this week," the nurse said. "Dr. Raines is filling in." When I explained my symptoms, she told me to go to bed to see if the cramping slowed down. If not, Dr. Raines could see me that afternoon.

Hesitantly, I hung up and went to bed, hoping and praying the cramping would end. Suddenly, I felt weak and nervous. Phil checked on me repeatedly as he prepared to go out of town for a concert.

By early afternoon, the cramping intensified, accompanied by bleeding. Phil dropped what he was doing and drove me to the doctor's office in Syracuse.

It was a long, silent hour. Neither of us wanted to speak our worst fears again.

We waited for what seemed like forever for the doctor to arrive. I quietly made repeated trips to the bathroom, losing clots of blood. I wanted to scream out in pain and frustration, "Would somebody please help me here? I'm losing this baby!" Instead, I painstakingly waddled into the examining room, waiting again for the doctor to show up. Phil sat with me, looking dumbfounded and helpless.

By the time Dr. Raines came in, I was ill from the pain and heavy cramps and he confirmed what was already obvious to us. "Mrs. Keaggy," he said, "by the looks of things you've already lost this baby. You're going to need a D&C to prevent infection and to make

---

From the journal of Lisa McMinn,
to baby Emma, lost to miscarriage…

You would be due any day now—maybe even today. Sweet child, how I wish to cradle you in my arms, to feel your breath on my neck, to nurse you at my breast. Why did God give you to me— a seed growing—but plucked before its time, wrenched out of my womb, out of my life? Dear Emma, I would have loved to love you.…All this just to say, I still hold you in my heart.

Facts About Miscarriage

- Most miscarriages occur when a pregnancy is not developing normally.

- Chromosomal abnormality is likely the cause of a first miscarriage in the first trimester of pregnancy.

- Other factors that contribute to first-trimester miscarriage include hormonal problems, infections, and the mother's health problems.

- Lifestyle choices that increase the risk of a first-trimester miscarriage include two or more alcoholic drinks per day, cigarette smoking, and three or more cups of coffee per day (or the equivalent amount of caffeine).

- Second trimester miscarriage is often caused by problems with the uterus or by a weakened cervix that dilates prematurely. As with first-trimester losses, maternal infections and chromosomal abnormalities can cause miscarriage.

—March of Dimes Web Site: www.modimes.org

Fiction About Miscarriage

The following does *not* increase the risk of miscarriage:
- Sex
- Working outside the home (unless a woman works with harmful chemicals)
- Exercise

—March of Dimes Web Site: www.modimes.org

sure the uterus is clear. I'll make arrangements for you
to be admitted to the hospital right away and schedule
your surgery for today."

I was in a daze as the nurse wheeled me out and
explained things to Phil. We were in a numbed silence—
no tears, simply trying to take in the disappointment.

After the nurse settled me into a hospital room, the
surgeon came in and introduced himself. He was an
older man with graying hair, and he had an easy, kind
manner. "This procedure will be painless," he said
softly. "We'll give you general anesthesia, and it will be
over quickly." I thought, *My body will survive—it's used
to pain now—but my heart is another story.* No one
could do anything for the agonizing emotional ache I
felt. There was no pill to lift my shroud of depression.
The surgeon left Phil and me alone for about an hour
until my surgery.

"How can I leave for the concert tonight with you
going into surgery?" Phil asked. But we both felt he
needed to honor his commitment and leave for New
Jersey. I was so used to his touring that I thought I
could handle this alone. Phil hugged me and reluc-
tantly left the hospital to make arrangements for a
friend to pick me up the next day.

I was alone that night in the hospital, alone with
my thoughts. I was afraid. I whispered to God, *"Are you
there? Help me. I can't do this alone."* Then the nurse
came in and wheeled me to surgery. The anesthesiologist started an IV, and soon the clear liquid running

Repeated Miscarriages

Many women who have experienced miscarriage worry they will miscarry again. But consider these statistics:

- Fortunately, at least 85 percent of women who have had one miscarriage will go on to have a successful pregnancy the next time, as will 75 percent of those who have experienced two or three losses.

- In about 25 percent of cases, the cause of repeated miscarriages cannot be found. However, couples in this situation should not lose hope: Even without treatment, about 60 percent of women with repeated miscarriages eventually have a healthy pregnancy.

—*March of Dimes Web Site: www.modimes.org*

into my vein blocked out any conscious thoughts. I awoke in yet another recovery room, thinking, *It's over and that is that.* Confusing thoughts filtered through my mind: *I can't even sustain a pregnancy long enough for the doctor to help me. I'm a failure.* I was tired of trying to figure out God, and my own life, for that matter. I just wanted to sleep.

The next morning a friend picked me up from the hospital and took me home with her for a couple of days, until Phil returned. Phil called often, anxiously checking on my condition. After a couple of days of being in that busy household, surrounded by children, I insisted I was well enough to go home.

That's when I hit bottom. I felt defeated. I had no more strength to fight. I was through with running this emotional and physical race. I cried out, "I give up. The ball's in your court, God. The set is over."

I went through the motions of each day. It was a struggle even to get out of bed. I had a hard time finding pleasure in anything. Cooking, which I loved, became a chore. It was depressingly cold and overcast outside, and I felt trapped and discontented. I tried reading Scripture, and that gave me some comfort. I reread the letters of C. S. Lewis, who said, "God, who foresaw your tribulation has especially armed you to go through it not without pain but without stain." Somehow I had to pick up my armor again and battle my way through this.

When Phil came home from the studio one day, we tried talking about our feelings. I told him I wanted to get out of the baby business. He agreed. We decided to put our dream of having children on the shelf. When I went back to see Dr. Harris for a checkup after surgery, I could tell he felt awful about what had happened. He wanted to help us, but I hadn't gone far enough in the pregnancy for him to do the procedures. "If and when you both feel it's right to try again, I'll be with you 100 percent," he said. I thanked him and left, feeling I was closing a chapter of my life.

Journal

Carry Your Sorrow No Longer

BY ELINOR MADEIRA

Carry your sorrow no longer
Give Him your burden to bear.
How we all long to dwell with Him
Now your child is already there.

And He says, "All you who are heavy laden
Oh, I will give you rest.
And I will lift you up
And you shall endure the test."

He mourns for the sheep who have lost their way
He weeps for those who have strayed.
He cries for all who are weary and old
But He rejoices when His children
come home to stay.

Carry your sorrow no longer
Give Him your burden to bear.
He's holding His child in His bosom
Remember He is love and He cares.[1]

Chapter Five

Good Grief:
Coming to Grips with Loss

Life went on, with or without me. I found that either you walk the path quickly or you stumble along with your feet dragging in the dirt. I was definitely stumbling along. Grieving.

Slowly, I forced myself back into the swing of things. Once again, we began to host the many single people in the community. And I enjoyed cooking for them and discussing life with them—as long as it didn't get too personal.

But at the same time, my anger troubled me, as my unanswered questions walled off my heart. I had trusted God with my dreams. And I had been crushed.

How I would have loved to sit down with someone who had gone through something similar—someone who could understand my feelings! If only I could have talked to a counselor and poured out my pain—without worrying whether he or she thought I was spiritual enough. I put up a great front around friends, so it was no wonder that everyone thought I was fine. I felt like no one had experienced such grief or loss themselves. After all, they were concentrating on life and living, not death and pain. But the fact remained: It hurt that no one sought me out when I most needed it.

Many nights when I'd finally fall asleep, I would have the same nightmare. I'm lying in the middle of this cold, sterile delivery room. Phil's by my side, smiling as we wait for the nurse to hand me our newborn son. "Here he is, Mrs. Keaggy, and he's beautiful!" the nurse exclaims. My hands reach out for him, all cuddled in the blue blanket. She stops suddenly, "Oh, there's been a mistake. Your baby's dead." She starts laughing hideously.

"My baby," I cry. "I want my baby."

"Darling, I have to go now, I'm late for a concert," Phil says, patting my hand. "You'll feel better tomorrow...."

Then I'd awaken both Phil and myself, screaming for them to bring my baby back. Sobbing and soaked in sweat, I would let Phil hold me and comfort me until I fell asleep.

For the most part, I kept my thoughts to myself, did my best to pull myself together after my losses, and went on. But deep down I felt guilty about my grief. I felt like a second-rate Christian, because my arms ached to hold my babies. What was the matter with me?

As I grieved the loss of my babies, I became aware that there was another emotion that dictated much of my life: fear.

When Phil was away traveling with the band, I constantly battled the anxiety of being alone. I often invited my friend Jacqueline to come and stay with me. I struggled with what I could control in my life and what I couldn't.

One night when Phil was gone and I lay in the bed alone listening to every noise, I became convinced someone was lurking outside the house, trying to find a way to get in. I was terrified.

Afterward, the depression was agonizing. I cried every day. What made it worse for me was that my sister was pregnant too. Her friends (unknowingly of course) even had a baby shower for her on my due date (I didn't tell anyone), which was incredibly painful for me to attend....Since my loss I have encountered so many others who have experienced pregnancy loss. I had no idea it was so common before it happened to me because people didn't talk about it...it helps so much to talk and cry.

EDYE DAMA
Lilburn, Georgia

Fear had woven itself into my life and was trying to paralyze me as I lay frightened in my bed. This was crazy! I felt angry at myself for being so controlled by my fears, angry enough to finally face it. I had built so many walls, trying to protect myself—but all I protected inside those walls was a fearful child, not the mature woman I wanted to become.

Anniversary Grief

Anniversary dates of your baby's birth, death, or due date may bring on a resurgence of grief, called the "anniversary reaction." As an anniversary approaches, you may deal with emotions ranging from tears to irritability to depression. Usually, after the anniversary has passed, the upset subsides.[1]

Suddenly, I was tired of it all. I cried out for God's peace and his assurance. I made a conscious decision: I would no longer be a prisoner in my own home—or a prisoner in my own heart. The words from Psalm 4:8 lulled me to sleep: *I will lie down and sleep in peace, for you alone, O LORD, make me dwell in safety.*

Maybe I was finally ready to accept that God's safety was not the smooth-sailing kind I'd been looking for. I was standing at the edge of a chasm. To go on with life, real life at a deep level, meant that I had to stay open to love. Without love, why be alive?

But to love seemed to mean risking more loss and more hurt. Why did these two things have to be linked together? I knew that to choose love and life gave me no guarantees.

C. S. Lewis wrote in *The Four Loves:* "To love at all is to be vulnerable." But, he warned, to lock your heart away from love—as I was tempted to do, thinking I could keep myself safe from hurt—was far more dangerous. He nailed me directly in the soul when he wrote:

> Love anything, and your heart will certainly be wrung and possibly be broken. If you want to make sure of keeping it intact you must give your heart to no one, not even to an animal. Wrap it up carefully round with hobbies and little luxuries; avoid all entanglements; lock it up safe in the casket or coffin of your selfishness. But in that casket—safe, dark, motionless, airless—it will change. It will not be broken; it will become unbreakable, impenetrable, irredeemable. The alternative to tragedy, or at least to the risk of tragedy, is damnation. The only place outside of Heaven where you can be perfectly safe from all the dangers and perturbations of love is Hell.[2]

Was that what I wanted—to go on living in a "safe hell" of my own making? Or would I risk again, become vulnerable, like clay in a potter's hands—maybe never be able to make my life the way I had always dreamed of it?

Lewis concluded, "If our hearts need to be broken, and if (God) chooses (the loss of someone we love) as the way in which they should break, so be it."[3]

I was tired of the fear. I was ready to admit that perhaps all the good things I tried to fortress my heart with—things that seemed good and joyful and of the light—were not the *ultimate* good, because they were

I grieve because something I have wanted so badly for so long has been taken away from me. I grieve because I didn't get to see what my children looked like. I grieve even for the future; the loss of first steps, birthday parties, graduations, and weddings. I even grieve that I'm simply not pregnant. I loved knowing that my body was nurturing a life. As bad as this all hurts, I have survived the worst days. I am more compassionate and sympathetic to others who grieve. My heart is more tender, and I hold life more precious. God did not abandon me through all of this. And, as hard as it is to believe at the moment, the pain does lessen with time. I will always love my babies, and there will always be a void in my heart for them, but the hurt does ease.

TINA FONDREN
Tuscaloosa, Alabama
After three miscarriages....
she's now the mother of Emily Lyndal.

not lasting. And maybe the events that I thought of as "dark" were just deep shakings to wake me up—love, of a totally different kind. *So be it.*

There was no going back. It was time to make a leap across this chasm that I'd come to in the floor of my soul.

After losing the triplets and Ryan, but before my miscarriage, Phil and I decided it might be helpful to put some of my creative energies into art classes. I enrolled in some noncredit art classes at Cornell University with my friend Linda. I was happy to discover a new outlet, especially a creative one, to pour my energies into—to feel like I was doing something, creating something. To feel like I was worthwhile, that I was important to God, to my friends, and to myself. I realized I had been struggling to believe it.

The Five Stages of Grief

Elisabeth Kübler-Ross names the five stages of grief in her book *On Death and Dying*.[4] Recognize these as a normal part of losing a child:

- Denial (This can't be happening!)

- Anger (How could a loving God allow this?)

- Bargaining (I'll do everything right, God, if I can have a child.)

- Depression (God has forgotten me.)

- Acceptance (I will go on with my life, even though I don't understand.)

Linda and I had great fun working on the potter's wheel and making copper and pewter jewelry. As I worked, I realized I was like this lump of clay in front of me. God was trying to mold me into something useful, beautiful. But I knew I was resisting the constant trickle of water he was adding to soften and shape me. Instead of opening myself to God, I was fighting—and as a result, I'd wound up feeling like a failure. *Maybe*, I thought, *it's time to stop resisting. Maybe I need to go to God for healing before this pain can be changed into something useful.*

Failure had done miserable things to my self-image. In my mind, I had failed again. Now I needed to go to God and realize that he loved me no matter what I had accomplished or hadn't accomplished in this life.

My emotions held me back. Guilt, failure, anger. The voice inside that said, *I'm not good enough.*

Was I ready for God to reshape me? I wasn't sure.

After the third pregnancy, Phil and I tried to pick up the emotional pieces and go on. But we were numb; every part of our lives seemed strained. We each retreated into our separate worlds. Our communication faltered as both of us felt unable to give each other what we needed.

Phil poured his energy into his music. But he was at a loss for words and so began expressing himself instrumentally, which eventually led to his album *Master and the Musician*. Sometimes music expresses our feelings in ways that words cannot. That's how Phil worked out his pain and confusion.

Physical Recovery

Your body needs time to recover after a loss—two weeks to a month or more. Most women will have a menstrual period four to six weeks after a miscarriage. As hormones, along with your uterus, are adjusting back to a pre-pregnant state, it's important to take care of yourself.

1. Eat healthy. Avoid extremes, such as comforting yourself with food to ease the pain or avoiding food altogether.

2. Get sufficient sleep. Your body needs it to recover. You may need to talk to your doctor for help if your grief is keeping you awake at night.

3. Slowly return to a regular exercise pattern (or begin a new one). It's amazing how even if you don't feel like exercising, working out with weights or doing something aerobic will make you feel better and be a good mood elevator. After I lost my babies, I began jogging. Often, I'd run hard and long until I'd feel sweat pouring down my skin. As I ran, I'd feel my pent-up emotions rise to the surface, and I'd let go of them. Even today, Phil and I take a brisk 40-minute walk twice a week in the park together, where we talk, share our feelings, and work out any problems we might be having.

4. Remind yourself that you are eating, sleeping, and exercising because you are important to God, your husband, and yourself!

5. Before you resume sexual activity, talk with your doctor and your husband about your emotional and physical health. Take into consideration whether you want to become pregnant again, and if so, how long you want to wait. Honest, open communication is crucial.

Emotional and Spiritual Recovery

1. Give yourself time—Expect to experience a multitude of emotions: crying, anger, etc. You may need some solitude to mourn your loss. Walk through your emotions, and slowly release them to God. He understands our weaknesses. He knows our sorrow. He's our only true confidant!

2. Sharing your pain—Do you feel frozen with grief? Unable to move on? Oftentimes others don't realize how much you are hurting. Although most people won't understand your grief, there will be those who will listen and support you. Choose wisely and carefully who you open your heart to. You may want to seek professional help from a pastor or counselor, or join a support group through your community, church, or hospital.

3. Fully embrace your grief—Give yourself permission to grieve. You will never forget your loss—and you are not meant to forget! Perhaps today you feel terrible. Tomorrow you might feel a little better. But let yourself feel.

4. Avoid blaming yourself or your spouse—Why me? What have I done to deserve this? Am I paying for my sins? Is this my fault? It's natural to think all of these thoughts. We live in a fallen world, and we are not exempt from suffering. We have to choose what to do with our feelings. Will they bury us? Or will they make us stronger? Choose to let your experience make you stronger.

5. Look to God for healing—Our God is a God of comfort and consolation. Go to his Word. Read Isaiah 43:2 and Psalm 40:1-3. Take little steps outside your grief, crack the door open a little bit at a time and let God's healing love and compassion enter in.

6. Use your experience to help others—Life is a journey. As we walk the road, we may find a chance to help someone else who is going through the same losses. By reaching out to others, we can often help heal ourselves.

7. Be thankful—Lay your burden down at the foot of the cross. Jesus is the ultimate comforter. He understands your pain as no one else does. God is in control of the universe, and he sees around the corner of your heart. Bless God at all times, and may his praise fill your mouth always, even in times of difficulty.

But I could find no outlet for my grief. Not that I didn't try! I frantically filled the void with art and dance classes, and with cooking for friends—anything to help fill the emptiness that I began to believe was permanent. I even turned to soap operas for an escape. I'd plan my day around getting home in time to see *One Life to Live.* The actors' problems seemed so constant and futile that it made me feel better about my own.

Before my third pregnancy, I still believed I was in control of my future. If I did certain things right, I thought, the outcome would be as I planned. The Scripture "In his heart a man plans his course, but the Lord determines his steps" (Proverbs 16:9) took on new meaning for me. For so long I had thought: *I'm healthy. I'm loving. There's no reason I should be denied the privilege of having a child.* When the doctor told me my physical problems could be treated, I thought there was no stopping us. It was humbling to realize that no matter how hard I tried, the result was in God's hands. I could not manipulate the outcome.

I began to realize that our faith does not mold God into what we want him to be. Our faith cannot force God to give us what we want, no matter how badly we want it. His mercy and love for us far outweigh what we may desire.

The more Phil and I discussed our experiences with others, the more we became convinced that we live in a pain-filled, fallen world. Any idea that we can, that we *should*, live an ideal life is a joke, a delusion.

I'd been pretty self-involved, thinking I was somehow specially singled out for disappointment. But pain and sadness were all around us, and I realized that every human being has a story to tell. Why had I been so blind to it before?

I felt my spirituality becoming more humanized, more *real* than I'd ever experienced before. It seemed to embrace all of life, all the human experience that lay between life and death.

And maybe, I thought, I could open the door to my soul again—just a crack—and venture out of myself once more. Had I really seen myself in the fires of sorrow? Had I received myself yet, my true self, from God? Or was I still Bernadette Keaggy, made in the image I wanted her made in?

Journal

Journal

Journal

Journal

Michael's Song

BY BECKI AND SCOTT HEDRICK

Oh Lord, I really need your comfort today,
My heart is heavy and inside I ache,
What once was filled with life is now a barren place,
I left here feeling empty and in need of your grace.
Dear Jesus please sing a sweet lullaby
To my baby I'll never hear cry.
Who will never lie close to my breast.
Gently cradle and give him rest.

Jesus, you're the only one who can heal this mother's grief
Whose hopes and dreams have vanished as if taken by a thief.
My soul has labored in sorrow, pain and tears,
So all I ask you Jesus is you hold my baby near.
Dear Jesus please sing a sweet lullaby
To my baby I'll never hear cry.
Who will never lie close to my breast.
Gently cradle and give him rest.

I sometimes wonder if his eyes are blue
What's he thinking now as he looks up at you?
Won't you tell him I love him and I'm waiting for the day
When my arms will hold him, but until then I pray
Dear Jesus please sing a sweet lullaby
To my baby I'll never hear cry.
Who will never lie close to my breast.
Gently cradle and give him rest.[5]

*Becki and Scott Hedrick of Wheeling, West Virginia,
lost their baby to miscarriage.*

Chapter Six

Coping with Well-Intentioned Family and Friends

So often after miscarriage or the loss of a child, friends and family don't know what to say. After Phil and I lost our first babies, people tried various forms of encouragement. Some of our friends avoided the subject altogether, afraid they'd upset me. In retrospect, I probably acted as if I was doing better than I really was.

Even worse than the silence were those who would say the wrong things. *"I thought you'd be over this by now." "Don't worry, you'll have other children." "All things work together for good...."* One woman, in an attempt to encourage me, said brightly, *"Oh, don't be upset. You'll get pregnant again."* I began to get a clear picture: People really didn't understand. These children who had died were my own flesh and blood. Even if we did have more children, they would never replace the five we lost.

Another friend said, "Your babies are in heaven. That's something to smile about."

Smile? Is that all that mattered—whether or not I could smile?

Words like these—well-intentioned, but painful nonetheless—can bring fresh agony to a mother's or father's heart that is already raw and bleeding.

One day in the grocery store I ran into Marie in the cereal aisle, trying unsuccessfully to appease her 2-year-old.

"Bernadette, how are you? Boy, kids can really be a pain," she said. "You'll know what I mean when you have them."

I forced a smile and quickly moved on. She had just added another stone to the wall around my heart.

On another occasion, after church, Nancy and Bob excitedly showed us their newborn baby, Zac. Nancy

---

It is not pleasant to have to inform someone that you've miscarried, and it also places the person in the awkward position of having to respond to that news. Oftentimes, in the absence of time to think clearly, things are said unintentionally that only serve to add to the pain, like, "I guess it just wasn't meant to be." This child was meant to be!

STEVE AND SANDY McMANUS
Lincoln, Nebraska

chirped as she plopped him in my arms that she was sure it would comfort me "since you never really got to hold your babies."

My hands felt weak and clammy, and it was all I could do to keep from dropping him.

After we lost our baby Noah Michael, who was stillborn at 38 weeks, we had people from our church calling to check on us and see how we were doing. Their input, support, concern, and love during that time was a total blessing for us.

REBECCA SCHROEDER
Littleton, Colorado

People offered us such trite phrases as "I guess it's not so bad when you know your children are in heaven. That's comforting, isn't it?" There was no comfort in these shallow words. I became more angry. I felt cynical and far away from God. How could a loving God allow this? I thought he loved me. I felt worthless and incapable.

When another well-meaning friend said, "I know God has a special plan in this for you and Phil," tears welled up in my eyes. What plan? I thought children were a part of his plan.

One morning, my friend Ellen and I sat in a little café drinking coffee. Out of the blue she asked, "Do you feel you've gotten over the miscarriages? Do you plan to get pregnant again?"

It caught me off guard, and the word *miscarriage* seared my emotions. My heart started pounding, and my blood pressure shot through the roof.

"Ellen," I said, trying to compose myself, "my first two pregnancies were not miscarriages, which happen in the first trimester—they were premature births. When you go into labor and deliver a two and one-half pound infant who lives for three days, that is *not* a miscarriage."

After Jared was stillborn I wanted so desperately to just return to my home. Why did they need to keep me overnight? The only reason new mommies stay in the hospital is to learn how to care for their babies. I felt like I was being held prisoner in a way. My baby was dead and I just wanted to go home. My heart has never ached so badly. It literally hurt. My husband called both sets of parents. I remember telling him to tell them not to make the 40-minute trip to the hospital. There was no baby to see, and I would be home tomorrow. Within the hour, they all arrived. I didn't realize how much I needed their hugs and support until I saw them.

SANDY FERGUSON
Rochester, New York

She was obviously embarrassed, and I backed off with a halfhearted smile.

"I'm sorry," Ellen said. "I was just concerned about you. I didn't realize it was still such a touchy subject. You seem to be adjusting so well."

It was true. My emotions could still become volcanic at a moment's notice, and I'd find myself off balance.

Healing is a slow, daily process, I learned, and there's no quick way out. I was glad for a friend like Ellen, who needed no façades, no apologies, no explanations.

Our friends all had different ways of expressing their love and concern. Some were deeply touching. After the loss of my triplets, Lonnie was one of the few who gave me what I needed. Fortunately, she came to see me soon after I got home from the hospital. "Hi, how are you feeling?" she asked cautiously.

"OK, I guess," I said, concealing the truth.

She handed me a small milk-glass vase, with peach silk flowers in it. "I'm sorry," she said.

Then she stood next to my bed, watching my tears flow, not knowing what to say. I knew she was hurting for me—I could see it in her eyes.

Then she said the most amazing thing: "It could have just as easily been me. I know that I don't understand it all either."

I think it was as hard for Lonnie to be around me as it was for me to see her still pregnant. From then on, she kept her thoughts of her pregnancy to herself and was sensitive to my feelings. I appreciated that. Lonnie had a compassion that reached out in total empathy. She wasn't afraid to approach me, even though I could see that it made her uncomfortable. She really wanted

---

From Kim Napier, whose daughter Mercy
died in utero on Christmas Eve…

We learned later the cord was around her neck twice. Although (the doctors) wanted to administer a fairly violent drug to induce an immediate delivery, Larry and I (wanted to wait)....During the weeks I carried Mercy after she died…people came out of the woodwork with "words from God." (Someone) told me, "God gave you four. He says this one is his." A couple we had never met heard about Mercy and came to our church to take us out to lunch to tell us it was our fault if Mercy was born dead because we were making a bad confession by saying she died....I was willing for God's will, but I was sick and very tired of his immature children putting words in his mouth and then in our ears. (Then God told me), "Pay no attention to these words, only to hearts. They come out of love." If I looked past mouths, I found people hurting with us, hoping to help.

KIM AND LARRY NAPIER
Thompsons Station, Tennessee

to understand the pain I was feeling, and I felt I could cry around her. I had many thoughts and feelings to work through. I kept that little vase of roses, because it symbolized a deep understanding of our loss.

Another friend, Elinor Hail, whose mother had committed suicide when she was 10 years old, shared with me how she found comfort and healing from her painful wounds when she gave Christ all the pain she'd been carrying.

"Not that it evaporated instantly—but I knew that I no longer had to carry that terrible weight alone. He was there, and when I turned to him I felt his comfort."

My brother-in-law and his wife lost a newborn after seven days. Anthony is a part of our family and will continue to be. Whenever a family quilt is made with grandchildren's names, his is there too. The value of family working together in prayer to support the grieving mother and father, to make every effort to include them in family activities to help heal and strengthen, goes a long way. Anthony's two brothers, who were 5 and 8 at that time, continue to remember him and are proud to have had another brother.

BOB HANNAH
No city given

Words and Actions That Comfort

Friends and family often ask how they can help you through this difficult time, because they aren't sure what support to offer. You may wish to either copy this page and give it to them or suggest some of the following:

1. Don't tell the parents you understand how they feel. Each loss is unique. Rather, be supportive by telling them you are sorry and you care. Offer to listen without giving advice.

2. Offer practical help. Are there other children in the family you can take out for the afternoon to give their mother time to rest and recuperate after her loss?

3. Fix some frozen dinners that can be put away for the times when the simple act of fixing a meal can seem overwhelming.

4. Offer to run errands or do basic household chores, such as throwing in a load of laundry or picking up dry cleaning.

5. Give the couple opportunity to talk about their loss. One of the most difficult things about losing a child is the feeling that others do not acknowledge that they existed.

6. Note the date that the miscarriage or stillbirth occurred, and remember to be extra sensitive when it rolls around the next year.

7. Holidays such as Mother's Day and Father's Day, baby showers, and family get-togethers may be a challenge for the couple after their loss. Respect their need for privacy while letting them know you want to be there for them. Encourage them not to withdraw, balancing their time for being with people with time for privacy and healing.

8. A short phone call just to let the hurting couple know you are thinking about them may be the ray of light in a dark day that keeps them treading water.

9. Slip the couple a gift certificate to a nice restaurant so that they can have a quiet evening out together.

10. Drop a note in the mail, reminding them that you care. You don't have to say anything profound, just show them your love.

I listened intently. In my anger and hurt, had I been turning to God—or turning away from him?

"Of course I wondered sometimes," Elinor said, "why God didn't in some way prevent Mom's death. I suppose he could have, because he's God. But I'll never know the answer to that, not in this life anyway. And I found that if I focused only on my loss, I was in danger of missing all the other things that God was doing in my family's lives."

Her story made me think. *While I'm holding on to this pain—and shutting myself off from God—what am I missing? What does he want to do in me that I'll lose if I don't learn to trust him more?*

Our experience of losing children gave us compassion for others who were in pain. It made us take our eyes off ourselves and reach out.

When Phil put together a new band for an upcoming tour, we got to know Jerry, the drummer, and his wife, Grace. When it was time for her to deliver, Grace gave birth to a full-term, stillborn child. My heart ached for them, as Jerry told us the news over the phone. Cautiously, I called Grace and shared in her pain and cried with her. Then I prayed for her. I encouraged her to call me whenever she needed someone to talk to. Many evenings, Grace did call. I suggested she write down her feelings—the good *and* the bad—to help her sort through her emotions. I also encouraged her to seek out a group of people who met through the local hospital to share their similar experiences and to comfort one another. I knew this was important because, as Paul reminds us, we are to "carry each other's burdens, and in this way you will fulfill the law of Christ" (Galatians 6:2).

The law of Christ is to love—even when it is difficult or uncomfortable.

How well I know these things. How much it cost to learn them.

It's easy to become caught up in our own lives and not look out for each other. The truth is, a five-minute phone call or a short note in the mail may be all that a desperate or lonely person needs that day to keep them from utter despair.

Why do we so quickly, easily, close off from others? Why do we forget that when someone is in the midst of difficulty and pain, survival becomes all-consuming? During those times, we can hardly see the dark cloud that surrounds us. We become incapable of dealing with our own needs. That's when we need true friends to be there for us, emotionally and in practical ways.

A small offer of love is all it takes to communicate, "You're special. You're important. You're worth taking the time for. You're not a failure."

There are inner lessons, of course, that we can learn only on our own. Part of growing up is learning that death is going to be a part of life. Often we simply refuse to deal with death, so we deny ourselves and others the time to grieve.

When our dear friend Bruce Coleman died—a slow, painful death—leaving behind his wife, Nancy, and two small children, our own experiences with loss gave us a small glimpse of what it must be like to lose a wonderful husband of many years. We empathized with Nancy and tried to help her in tangible ways. During the months following Bruce's death, we talked often—any time, day or night, that she needed to. We shared dinners and went for walks. Sometimes, when fear and loneliness became too much to bear, Nancy and the children spent the night with us in our home.

The healing process, we knew, is as slow and painful as death itself. After the initial trauma,

everyone else seems to move on with their lives—
everyone but you. Too often we can try to quickly fill
that loveless void with something else. But God works
on our hearts in a much slower, unique pattern—if we
allow him to.

Journal

Journal

Journal

Disappointment

BY PHIL KEAGGY

Disappointment—HIS appointment, change one letter,
Then I see, that the thwarting of my purpose
is God's better choice for me.
His appointment must be blessing,
though it may come in disguise,
For the end from the beginning, open to His wisdom lies.

Disappointment—HIS appointment, whose?
The Lord's who loves me best,
Understands and knows me fully,
Who my faith and love would test.
For like a loving, earthly parent,
He rejoices when He knows,
That His child accepts unquestioned
all that from His wisdom flows.

Disappointment—HIS appointment,
Lord I take it then as such,
Like the clay in hands of pottery
yielding wholly to Thy touch.
All my life's plan is Thy molding,
not one single choice is mine,
Let me answer unrepining
Father not my will but Thine.[1]

from the poem "Disappointment" by Edith Lillian Young

Chapter Seven

Marriage and Loss

When you lose a child, your marriage is disrupted. But the grief and disappointment you feel, and the readjustments you have to make with your spouse and your family, are surmountable. Studies show that although it is clear parents who have suffered through the death of a child experience more distress than a normal couple, it isn't true that the marriage will inevitably fall apart. In *Parental Loss of a Child*, it is noted that "the notion that the stress of childhood illness and/or death automatically leads to divorce only exacerbates the pressure already felt by parents in such situations." The book goes on to say studies have found more than half of bereaved couples became more expressive of feelings and felt a sense of personal growth, and nearly two-thirds experienced an increased sense of spirituality. According to the book, couples also reported a heightened sensitivity to others, closer relationships, and a commitment to living life more fully and meaningfully because of their child's death.[1]

Of course, grieving your loss together takes time. After the loss of the triplets and Ryan, Phil and I escaped any way we could. We hung out often with friends and watched old movies—anything to avoid the truth that pain and suffering were part of the larger picture of our lives.

We began to shut down emotionally with each other. We had trusted that this time everything would work out, and we had been trampled on—worse than the first time. Our relationship became stifled. We didn't know how to help each other anymore. Phil and I both struggled to find our own outside sources of comfort, as well as other people to help satisfy the void.

We were able to hold our 32-week-old son's tiny body for a brief time, wrapped tightly up in the small blanket and little cap that newborns wear. We marveled at his small fingers the way we had with our other children. We saw in his face the family resemblance. And we mourned the death of our son John.

BILL AND LIZ YATES,
parents of Seth, Isaac, Noah, and Mary
Annandale, Virginia

It was a difficult time in our marriage. Although we still loved each other, the years of emotional pain had strained our relationship. Our opinions on life were no longer the same—something that bothered Phil more than me. Phil was more accepting of what we'd been through, while I seriously questioned everything I believed about God. Phil's faith seemed

---

From Ken, whose son Jared was stillborn…

The hardest thing I have ever faced as a husband is seeing my wife, Sandy, consumed in grief and not being able to do anything to spare her from it.…During this time we attended Jared's memorial service, accepted the love, prayers, and hot meals of our wonderful church family.…However, our evenings were long, occasionally, when the initial flood of visitors dried up. I have heard it said that losing a child either strengthens a marriage or utterly destroys it. I am grateful that Sandy and I can say the experience served as an additional tie that binds. Despite that pain and mourning, we both felt that the other was the only one we could fully depend on to understand our down moments. I am grateful for God's protective hand.

KEN FERGUSON
Rochester, New York

stronger than mine, and he believed all our pain would somehow work out for good. After all, the death of his mother brought him to his first spiritual awakening and changed his life radically. Losing his mother while still in his teens had both toughened and mellowed Phil. *He* wasn't demanding answers to questions that, as far as he could see, would never be answered in this life. So I found myself searching for my own spiritual identity, apart from Phil—a good thing, but frightening, too.

When we lost our fifth child, I felt myself growing even further away from Phil. I could tell that Phil felt the distance too. We had to face the fact that we were basically non-confronters. We both had a way of holding in our negative thoughts and anxieties, hoping they'd go away.

For Phil and me, part of the healing process for our marriage came after reading Sheldon Vanauken's beautiful book *A Severe Mercy*. Vanauken wrote to C.S. Lewis in hopes of gaining some understanding of his grief after the painful death of his wife, Davy. Lewis had just lost his wife, Joy, to cancer, and the book is full of the letters they exchanged. Lewis wrote to Vanauken:

> I am sure it is never sadness—a proper, straight, natural response to loss—that does people harm, but all the other things, all the resentment, dismay, doubt and self-pity with which it is complicated.[2]

I related to this wholeheartedly. It was true that nothing and no one in my Christian experience encouraged me by acknowledging that my sadness was normal. But on the other hand, my sorrow was all bound up with other, more destructive responses, like resentment and doubt.

Lewis went on to say,

> Some people turn away from grief, go on world cruises or move to another town. But they do not escape, I think. The memories, unbidden, spring into their minds, scattered perhaps over the years. There is, maybe, something to be said for facing them all deliberately and straight away.[3]

Again, he had put his finger on the right issue. I had been thinking it would be easier to check out— physically and emotionally—in my relationship with Phil. And here was Lewis, challenging me to see that this was perhaps the worst response in the long run. To face my grief "deliberately and straight away"—was I brave enough to do that?

For his part, Vanauken's honesty was also deeply freeing and refreshing. There was no pretense of denial. Grief, he said reflectively, is also a form of love. He spoke of it as "…the longing for the dear face, the warm hand. While it lasts, grief is a shield against the void."[4]

These words brought up that old issue for me of self-protection. That tendency to build strong, inner walls—as if I could protect myself against all harm, as if I could keep my dreams and hopes and longings safe within me until I could make them real.

If I walked through this door of sorrow, which had obviously been opened up before me, what would I stand to lose? And what would I find on the other side? This was as scary as it was life-giving. I could choose to go on, with the hope of walking out of my inner pain in some way and at some point.

After Phil and I read *A Severe Mercy* aloud together, it gave us an opening to discuss our marriage and to talk about our future. Phil and I realized we had to face our pain honestly together. We had to accept the fact that pain and loss were changing our lives and our marriage.

We were not exempt from life's frailties. We had to make the choice to embrace our experiences and use

---

From Linda, whose baby girl was stillborn...

While I would never ask to have something like this happen in my life, I am glad that God allowed me to go through this valley, because it brought me ever so much closer to him and showed me how I could trust him in any circumstance.

LINDA (AND JOEL) BENSON
Neenah, Wisconsin

them to benefit others, and to learn about life from an eternal standpoint.

Phil and I talked about the way tragedy helps us find out what we are really made of, about when the essence of what we believe is shaken. It is a bit like God

---

Since others really avoided talking about what had happened...we buried our pain. My husband is the most patient, loving, godly man. We are so one in our walk with the Lord. But neither one of us knew how to handle this....I knew I needed to let it go and give every aspect of this to my Heavenly Father—the longing for my babies, the frustration from well-intentioned but hurtful remarks, the need for comfort, and the hope that I'd see them again one day. I slowly opened up and my husband and I did talk it through. I felt washed with Jesus' amazing love and comfort.... I've been able to comfort others a little, now that I've come out of the valley....We don't know what will happen tomorrow, but we know our Lord will be there with us.

ROBERTA NAHAS
*Roberta and her husband Dean
have gone through two miscarriages.
They now have three children.*

---

allowing Satan to test Job, time and again. He shook Job to the core of his being to see if he would still stand and trust God.

In reading the Vanaukens' story and how their love was tested, we realized that our pain and loss could destroy us—or it could make us stronger.

Phil and I turned to the Bible and read in Romans:

> The creation waits in eager expectation for the sons of God to be revealed. For the creation was subjected to frustration, not by its own choice, but by the will of the one who subjected it, in hope that the creation itself will be liberated....We know that the whole creation has been groaning as in the pains of childbirth right up to the present time (Romans 8:19-20,22).

These verses broadened my perspective of what it means to live in a world of pain and disappointment. Phil and I found some common ground—our hurt—where we could meet again, as well as the desire to hold on to some bit of our faith, however small it was for me at the moment.

Settling some of these issues in my mind allowed me to once again look beyond myself and evaluate what was happening around me. I saw that Phil and I had started looking more to other people for strength, friendship, and encouragement instead of turning to one another. My time with my single friends was an escape from reality for me. Phil spent more hours with his buddies in the band because I no longer listened to him or reached out to him. Our emotional oneness was gone, and I wanted it back.

One night, as Phil practiced his guitar in the small room off our bedroom, I went to him.

Mending Your Marriage

Be sure to spend time working on whatever cracks the (loss) caused in your marriage.... (Making) sure your marriage is healthy and on a proper track is important before you try to conceive again.[5]
—Dr. Lynn Friedman, M.D.

"We've got to talk," I said. He looked up at me, his eyes filled with pain. "I know we do," he said, setting his guitar aside and making room for me next to him.

My heart pounded as I said what I had already rehearsed in my mind a number of times: "I'm sorry, honey, that I haven't been here for you as a wife or a friend."

"We've always said we would be honest with God, with ourselves, and with each other," he quietly replied. "We've lost sight of that, haven't we? I'm so sorry we've allowed all these experiences to separate us." We held each other and cried, each one asking the other for forgiveness for letting our own selfishness rule our lives. I felt the stony corners of my heart start to dissolve.

Phil and I not only returned to the basics in our relationship, but we also watched it deepen. There were choices in our lives that we had to make. We needed to gain some perspective on our grief. I was caught up in the painful losses of our children, and Phil was very preoccupied with his career. We needed to devote some time to taking a hard look at our lives. This in itself was a fight—my tendency after each loss was to pull into myself. When I did, real, ongoing communication between Phil and me died. We knew we were going to have to fight against all the emotional trauma that had separated us. At the bottom of it all we had to fight for our marriage, to battle this together.

An unhappy woman usually needs a change of heart more than circumstances.

Our relationship was maturing. We decided it was OK to have differing opinions, that it was actually healthy and helped us make better decisions together. We were confident enough in each other's love to respect each other's individuality. We felt that even if we never had children—a good possibility—we were important enough to God and to each other to continually work on our marriage.

After that night, we started setting aside time together, away from the house, where we could have each other's undivided attention. The fact was that Phil and I did not share much of our everyday lives as a couple. The date nights we had were good, but we didn't have a lot of shared interests to talk about. We were living separate lives together.

We determined to find a shared pastime to rekindle our closeness and enthusiasm for being together. Phil enjoyed running and had even run a marathon. I decided I could enter his world a little more by taking up jogging.

We made time to take our first real vacation since our honeymoon and planned a 12-day trip to Hawaii. As the plane lifted off, I looked closely at Phil as he sat next to me. The hair at his temples was starting to gray. He was as thin and taut as ever, but the years of traveling and stress were showing in tiny lines around his eyes. Yes, I was still in love with this man. And I was grateful to have this time with him. *Life is so fragile, so much out of our control*, I thought.

Mornings in Hawaii, I combed the beaches for shells and sea life, taking in the warm tropical air while Phil caught up on his sleep. At lunchtime, we'd go out and discover out-of-the-way restaurants together. Then we'd ride bikes past acres of sugarcane and soak in the sun's rays on the sandy white beaches. I understood why people called this place paradise—not only for its amazing beauty but for what it does to you inside. I felt happy and free. No one knew us, and we could be ourselves without having to meet anyone's expectations. We made the most of each glorious day, laughing together and rediscovering our love for one another.

I thought about how dead set I had been about controlling our future. I had insisted that God work within the goals I had for my life. Now I yearned for a simpler spirituality, one that allowed me to accept my frail humanity, my weaknesses, and let God be God. I was tired of trying to live within a formulated Christianity that kept God in a box—a box controlled by me. It was so upside down, really. Find your dream or goal, pray for it, and poof—God, like a genie in a bottle, gives you what you want. Where did God our Maker, God the Sovereign One, come in?

When Phil and I returned to New York, in many ways we were different people. We had crossed a threshold I couldn't name. But our love for each other felt freer, less weighed down by expectations and demands. The same was true of our love for God. We were ready to stop *performing* for him and to simply rest in his goodness, no matter what. We were not so intent on getting what we wanted and a little more ready to let God carry us through whatever he might have for us.

It wasn't easy, because our friends' families were growing. Almost everywhere we went we saw children laughing, crying, clinging to their mothers' knees. That pulled on our heartstrings, and we felt we were missing out. But we accepted that a family was not in God's plan for us at this point in our marriage.

Journal

Journal

Journal

One Heart One Life

BY JERRY AND SANDI RECTENWALD

Oh, how can one heart feel so much love
That it breaks just at the thought of you?
And how can one life be so very brief?
Yet so profound that it changes the world?

It is a mystery to me, the miracle of life;
We are a part of something larger than we know.
You've opened places in our hearts
we never knew were there.
And we are amazed at the love that overflows.

When you came into his world,
we greeted you with joy.
You were the focus of so many hopes and dreams.
But this world greeted you with pain
that we couldn't take away.
I guess the mystery is deeper than it seems.

Yes, there are mysteries we don't want to know,
Places of pain we'd rather not go
And we have walked that dark path
with you, little one.

But I know there will come a day
When we'll walk hand in hand
In love and together evermore.

*Written by a father to his daughter Abby,
who was born at 24 weeks, and died prematurely.*

Chapter Eight

Just for Husbands
A Special Note for
Husbands—from Phil Keaggy

Often, after miscarriage or stillbirth, the grieving husband/father is forgotten. Men usually do not express themselves as openly as women do. They may feel clueless about how to help their wives—and their wives may not know how to let them help! Marriages may go through a time of difficulty and readjustment. Men may go through feelings of helplessness. It may be challenging to know how to tune into a wife's feelings, as well as for her to know how to let you in.

Husbands, you need to grieve to heal. You antici-pated being a dad—loving, caring for, teaching, and raising a child—and now your hopes are dashed. After we lost our first babies, I felt like a displaced father. One day, I was telling my friends I was going to be a papa, the next day I was not. I never even had the chance to see the triplets—my first sons.

When you lose a child through miscarriage or stillbirth, your marriage may go through a difficult, rocky season. This is a time to be all that you said yes to when you said your marriage vows before God and man.

> Then Jacob tore his clothes and put on sackcloth. He mourned deeply for his son for many days. His family all tried to comfort him, but it was no use. "I will die in mourning for my son," he would say, and then begin to weep (Genesis 37:34-35 NLT).

As Bernadette and I walked through the losses of our children together, I tried to be a comforter to the woman I'd grown to love so much. To be strong for her, praying constantly all hours of the night when fear and disappointment would rage. But I didn't always have the strength she needed. I needed strength for myself as well!

Anger, hopelessness, disappointment, confusion, hurt, sadness, failure, helplessness. I dealt with all these emotions and more. Most people found it safer to ask Bernadette how she was doing. Very few asked me how I felt.

Men tend to pour themselves into work as a way of dealing with grief. I took comfort in my music, yet I realized there was a part of me that had died. I lost confidence in my singing. I felt fragile. I wore my disappointment with quiet resignation.

In *A Woman Doctor's Guide to Miscarriage,* Dr. Lynn Friedman points out that men are socialized to go back to work after the loss of a child and not think about their own feelings. A man may feel like a failure as a man because he was not able to protect his wife from the loss and the ensuing emotional pain it caused her. And the husband, she writes, tends to think he has to solve all of his wife's problems.[1]

Losing a child is not a problem you can solve. Rather, it's a chance to support each other through a difficult time. Both of you will need a chance to heal.

Men, if you have lost a child, it's important to:

- give yourself permission to cry and to grieve the loss of your baby

- talk about your emotions with a close friend, pastor, or counselor

- keep the lines of communication open, and be ready to discuss your feelings with your wife and talk about your grief

- remember that work can be a good distraction and a relief (I'm accomplishing something!), but it isn't a complete solution to sadness and pain

- pray, even when you feel God is silent, or you can't find the right words

Listen to your wife with an open heart and try not to fill in the silence of her sorrow with well-intentioned words. Be her protector. Give her the gift of gentle understanding. Respect her way of grieving, which may be different from yours. She may just need you to be there for her—emotionally, physically, spiritually—supporting her in the healing process. Guard your marriage. Place it in a very protected space.

From the father of Carole Irene,
stillborn after 36 hours of labor...

After nine months of anticipation, all we were left with was a photograph and the sounds of other babies crying from the hallway. I was in such great sorrow and everything around me was status quo and I felt alone, as if absolutely no one cared, especially God....After arriving home, I sat on the step and I exploded. I cried and I screamed at God, wanting to know "why" this had happened....It took some time to get over my feeling that I never wanted to have kids (again). I still do not understand why God took Carole from us, but I am confident that he cares for us and truly wants the best for his children.

JAMES KAMMIN
Oak Lawn, Illinois
James and his wife, Ev,
now have three children:
Rosemary, Emily, and Carl.

You and your wife share a common brokenness. Take it to God. He is the healer of broken hearts, not the preventer.

From Ken, whose son Jared was stillborn…

I walked through the silent, dark house alone. I had gone all day trying to be strong for my wife, Sandy, so that I could make rational decisions as they were called for. I hesitated outside Jared's room, the nursery that we had rushed to finish in time for his fast-approaching arrival. I arrived at the foot of the crib with every intention of praying to God for strength, wisdom, acceptance of his will, and desire to see the good in his decision. I prayed half a sentence, "Lord, I don't understand but…" when a sob of monstrous proportions welled up in my chest. All the pain I had tried to hold at bay all day suddenly spewed up with such violence that my body shook and collapsed to the floor. I had a feeling of having my heart literally ripped from my chest cavity. I laid there, in the fetal position, crying as if I would never be comforted. When my body was too exhausted to cry anymore, I continued to lie silently at the foot of the crib. "God, where were you today? How could you let this happen?"

KEN FERGUSON
Rochester, New York

Affirm your wife. In God, you complete each other. Your family may grow, but perhaps not in the time and way you expected.

Show your love for your wife. Speak sincere words of devotion and commitment to her. Let her see your earnest desire to be the husband you were chosen to be. Read the Scriptures together. Pray for each other. Pray his Word together. Learn to be thankful in the

I am writing this from the often forgotten partner's point of view. My wife, who was three months into her first pregnancy, was taken to the hospital, where she experienced a miscarriage. Things happened around me, out of my control. I felt helpless to help my wife. I was excluded from the medical process by the "professionals" and only got to see Pauline after the D&C. The fetus was disposed of—we didn't know the sex or anything. It was cold, clinical. There was no counseling. It just happened. Then I had to take control at home—answering the telephone, receiving messages of sympathy, trying to be strong for Pauline. We christened the baby "Henry" and talked about him afterward.

STEVEN BRIDGE
Kent, England

midst of pain and sadness. Praise and thanksgiving are necessary even when we don't feel like it.

It's easy to withdraw from friends, family, and our church community. Don't isolate yourself! Friends are

My wife gave birth to our first children, twins Sunshine Joy and Katelyn Joy, on June 25th. However, they were born three months early. Sunshine lived only about 15 minutes after birth, and Katelyn was rushed off to intensive care. This experience has tested our faith in God and each other like nothing I have ever experienced. Katelyn was able to come home and is off all monitors and progressing nicely in her development. She is a blessing from God, and we continue to thank God for her every day. However, my wife, Summer, and I still struggle day to day with the emotions of losing Sunshine. I especially struggle with how to help my wife, who struggles with the emotions on a deeper level than I do. I am the youth pastor at our church, and the position of leadership puts us on a pedestal that is hard to live up to sometimes. Everyone expects us to be past the experience and ready to go on with life. It's kind of an unspoken thing, if you know what I mean.

JOSH FISHER
Howard City, Michigan

often afraid to "butt in" when you are walking on such
fragile ground. The burden of contact may fall on you.

Allow joy to come in. Joy is deeper than laughter,
deeper than happiness. True joy will help you find
happiness and contentment.

At the same time, allow yourselves to let the tears
flow as they must. And now and then let them mingle
as the two of you are one in him.

Journal

Journal

All Our Wishes

BY PHIL KEAGGY

All our wishes can't be wrong,
all these dreams between us two.
There are others who know this song,
who know the meaning of its tune.

He kneels by her side,
places his hand where there was life.
This child this baby is gone.
She hears him say, "We'll carry on."

All our wishes can't be wrong,
all these dreams between us two.
We are not the only ones,
though it seems it's me and you.
Yet for now it's me and you...[2]

Chapter Nine

Finding Grace: Children at Last

Two years had passed since my last pregnancy, and motherhood was again tugging at me. With the right medical attention, we felt we had to give it one last try before we resorted to other options, such as adoption.

By now, Phil and I had decided that sometimes you have to step out and trust God, no matter what. Not that the outcome is guaranteed to be wonderful. But we knew he would be there for us if we fell again. I now believed the outcome of this pregnancy was already determined—and certainly not by me.

We also made a decision to move. After solidifying our plans, we flew to Kansas City to look for a new home and to check out a good doctor. Within a week, we had found a lovely old stone house for sale, and the down payment matched Phil's royalties from his record company. I was ecstatic over owning our first home, and I pictured the changes we would make after it was ours.

While we were in Kansas City, I also called the
hospital connected with the local university and asked
for recommendations about doctors. Several sources
led me to Dr. Charles King, whose forte was dealing
with high-risk pregnancies. I called and made an
appointment to see him when we returned for good.

Within a matter of weeks, we were in our new
home. We had not even unpacked, however, when we
set off for New Zealand and Australia. Phil was scheduled to perform a couple of weeks of concerts and a
music seminar, and I was along for the ride. I felt
determined to not let this pregnancy, or my fears, keep
me from joining Phil in this experience. The doctor
couldn't do anything for me anyway until my fourth
month, so if something happened sooner, I felt it was
out of my control.

In New Zealand, we were welcomed by our gracious hosts, David and Dale Garrett, who knew the
meaning of true hospitality. They lavished loving care
on us as we stayed in their home during the first week
of our travels. Phil's concerts were well received, and
we felt enriched by our time in these lovely countries.

And inside, I felt that something was different—
truly different—about this pregnancy.

Upon returning to Kansas City, we went about the
task of unpacking boxes—and enjoyed it! With our
friends' help, we tore out old orange shag carpeting
and refinished the beautiful wood floors underneath.
Phil scraped off layer upon layer of old wallpaper, and
I, quite contentedly, picked out a new pattern.

My belly started to bulge once again, and those small first flutters of life became real and precious. It was once again a walk of trust for us, and we took it day by day. We came to appreciate the loving care and skill of Dr. King as he cautiously monitored my pregnancy. When we made it to the surgery at the end of my fourth month, I felt relieved.

As Phil checked me into the hospital and got me settled in my room, I felt uneasy. The anesthesiologist came in to give me a spinal block, and I thought back to all my dreadful hospital experiences in the past four years. *Today's experience could be just as bad,* I thought. *This procedure could either help bring life or cause me to miscarry.* But we were willing to take the chance, and I would not give in to fear.

Phil was by my side in surgery as Dr. King sewed a tiny purse-string suture around my cervix, then pulled it tightly closed. With only mild discomfort, I was back in my hospital room within the hour. These stitches would stay in until it was time to deliver.

Dr. King came into my room after surgery. "Everything went well," he said, " and we'll keep you overnight to make sure labor hasn't been induced. But the chances are slim. This procedure will bring on labor in about 5 percent of the cases—and hopefully you won't be one of them."

Hopefully, I thought.

The next day I was released from the hospital. I was told to take it easy, but I was not confined to bed. We'd crossed a major milestone, one step at a time.

Without God, life is utterly meaningless. Our times are in his hands. Consider this passage from the Old Testament:

"There is a time for everything, and a season for every activity under heaven...." (Ecclesiastes 3:1).

Phil and I chuckled together as my silhouette grew huge. How could I stretch another inch?

I still had to battle some old fears and some new ones. *Surely, something was going to burst this bubble,* I thought. *Don't get too excited. What makes you think this pregnancy will have a happy ending?*

Daily, I fought this battle with cynicism and fear, but deep down I wanted to believe God would give me this child.

As I passed my eighth month, I realized that this child had a good chance to make it. But what if something went wrong right at the end? I shared my fears with Phil, and he understood. We decided that God had brought us this far, and he would give us the child he wanted us to have. There was that challenge again—*to trust completely, no matter what.*

In the early hours of the morning, on March 19, 1980, I was awakened by annoying, consistent contractions. The baby wasn't due for three more weeks.

Around 5 A.M., I decided to call Dr. King at home. He told us to meet him at the hospital. We fumbled around the house, not quite prepared, and made our way out the door to St. Joseph's Hospital.

It was comforting to be met by Dr. King, who was waiting for us, calm and smiling. He examined me and snipped the cervical stitches. Then I was in full labor.

Phil and I walked the halls, pacing back and forth. *How ironic,* I thought. *After all this time of holding on to this pregnancy, this baby is going to come when it's good and ready.*

We spent the next hours in nervous anticipation. Phil and I walked and talked until the contractions were close and hard. Was this child really going to be ours—to keep and raise? Was it a boy or a girl? Who would it look like? The last stage of labor was long and slow, unlike the other pregnancies. Phil coached me through the breathing process, and as the pain grew more intense, I held onto him.

Our friends came in and out, cheering us on. At one point, I asked our good friend Paul to remove himself and his video camera from the room. I didn't want to have to look back and see myself sweating and panting furiously. Not a pretty sight!

Finally, the nurse announced it was time to head into the delivery room. I felt numb and strange. Phil talked loudly to get my attention. The monitor showed the baby's heartbeat begin to drop, and the nurse became agitated. "Come on Bernadette—push with this contraction!" the doctor ordered. Phil grabbed my

"I waited patiently for the LORD; he turned to me and heard my cry" (Psalm 40:1).

right arm and the nurse grabbed my left, and they added support as I pushed with all my strength.

"*I can't do it!*" I cried. But another contraction was already upon me.

"*Now,* Bernadette, make this count," Dr. King said. "You can do it!"

Frantically, I looked around between breaths. "Where's Phil?" He was still holding my hand, but he'd dropped to his knees, pleading for God's assistance and mercy.

And with that assurance, I squeezed his hand and pushed the baby out with all the strength I had left.

"*I see a head! I see shoulders!*" Dr. King shouted as he gently eased the child out.

There was no cry.

Dr. King quickly suctioned the baby's mouth and began rubbing its back vigorously. The silence was intense. Then he turned her over—her—our little girl. I heard the most wonderful sound. My little girl began to cry.

Our first daughter—and our sixth child, Alicia Marguerite Keaggy, was alive and healthy.

When I finally got to hold my baby, it was as if a piece of heaven and earth were wrapped up snugly within my arms. Tears rolled down our cheeks.

Later, when I was settled back in my room, they brought Alicia in, all cleaned up and wrapped in pink. Phil laid her on the bed, and we lovingly examined every inch of her 5-pound, 9-ounce little body—so beautiful and perfectly formed. We were in awe of God's creation before us.

My husband, Steve, and I were expecting our first baby. Everything went wonderfully until about 38 weeks. I went in for a routine checkup in June of 1994, and the doctor couldn't find the baby's heartbeat. After induced labor, Noah Michael was stillborn and weighed 5 pounds, 15 ounces. In January of 1995, I found out I was expecting again. Around 10 to 12 weeks I started bleeding and found out I was miscarrying twins. In May of 1995, I again was pregnant. At 33 weeks, my non-stress test showed something abnormal. Finally, on January 11, 1996, the doctors decided the baby's lungs were developed enough to induce labor. Seth Richard was born a month early, but healthy. It was a great feeling to walk out of the hospital with a baby—finally!

REBECCA SHROEDER
Littleton, Colorado

I didn't feel at all awkward or clumsy with her, but like a well-rehearsed athlete finally getting to play the real game. Phil handled this tiny one as if he'd been a papa for a very long time. She captured our hearts as I held her close and nursed her for the first time. How amazing that she instinctively knew what to do.

As is common in newborns, Alicia became jaundiced. My heart ached as I watched her under the lights with cotton patches taped over her eyes. Dr. King explained the necessity of this until her liver started functioning properly. By the fourth day, though, I was told it might be best to stop nursing for a few days and go home, leaving Alicia until her condition cleared up.

No way, I thought. I was determined not to leave that hospital without her. Dr. King understood.

On the eighth day, Alicia's bilirubin count dropped to safe levels, and we packed up and headed home. We were a family. We felt privileged to be one.

As we went through our first weeks and months with Alicia, I realized how much had changed inside of us. We lived with a new resolve that God really was sovereign—with a wisdom far beyond ours. Even when things do not turn out exactly as we hope, we can rest in knowing that, somehow, it is part of his bigger plan.

I wanted to guard my heart now and not let it close off again in a self-satisfied little world of motherhood. Maybe God's purpose in allowing all our losses was about to come clear. If so, I didn't want to miss it.

As time passed, Phil and I were happy to discover that I was pregnant again. Alicia was 3 years old at the time, and we felt she was ready to be dethroned, or at least to have a little companion at her side. But just because I had successfully given birth to Alicia didn't mean this time would be the same.

I walked through it cautiously, taking it a day at a time. My inward battle between trust and fear intensified during the second trimester. To top it off, we were moving again—this time to California. It meant packing and traveling and added stress.

We lost four children to miscarriage over the years. The first time, Vanessa was in her fourth month and went through full labor and transition at home. It was very traumatic. Being young and immature, I really did not know how to minister to her during that time. God did bless us with two beautiful children, including a 3½-year-old girl we adopted from the Philippines. The Philippine government questioned us about why we would want to adopt, and because we had so many miscarriages, they understood. So once again we can see how only God can bring life out of death.

PAUL AND VANESSA GRIMSLAND
Kingston, New York

Dr. King searched out one of the best high-risk pregnancy specialists in Orange County, California, and once we'd moved, I went to meet with him. Dr. Goldstein would do my surgery and monitor my pregnancy. This time I required higher dosages of drugs and more bed rest, but we made it through.

In my eighth month—on February 14, 1984— Olivia Anne, a gift from God, was born. We felt it significant that Olivia was born fourteen years to the day after Phil's mom was in a car accident that took her life. Each year, Valentine's Day holds a double meaning for us—that life is taken away, but it is also given as a good gift from a Father who loves us.

After Olivia's birth, the doctor cautioned us about future pregnancies being more difficult. By God's grace, we were blessed with a second child, and we were more than content. We had no desire to push the limits to have a third.

So I was shocked when, in the fall of 1986, the nurse in my doctor's office called to tell me the results of the tests the doctor had ordered. "Mrs. Keaggy," she said, "the tests are positive. You're pregnant."

I was stunned. I hung up the phone without saying a word.

As I sat down heavily at the kitchen table, I faced that old tendency to want to seize control. *I don't want to go through all the emotional turmoil again. I can't deal with this.* It wasn't the thought of a third child that bothered me; it was the process of getting there that had become, each time, a more serious undertaking.

Getting Pregnant Again

Medically speaking, it is considered safe to conceive after you have had one normal menstrual period (if you are not undergoing tests or treatments for the cause of your miscarriage). But before you decide to try to get pregnant again, ask yourself these questions:

- Are you physically ready? Some women should consult a specialist before they attempt to conceive. Is your body healthy enough to go into another pregnancy? Are you eating well again and taking care of yourself?

- If you have had two or more miscarriages (and especially if you are over age 35), or if you have an illness (such as diabetes or systemic lupus erythematosus) that can affect your pregnancy, or if you have had fertility problems, you should see an expert in high-risk pregnancy.

- Are you emotionally ready? It's normal to feel depression, exhaustion, a sense of failure, and shock after you miscarry or lose a child. Only you can determine when your grief has eased and you are ready to welcome another child. Be sure your emotional health has been restored—and that you are not trying to immediately replace this loss with another pregnancy.

- Another pregnancy should be the result of a careful decision that you and your husband make together.

- Consider the spiritual aspects of another pregnancy. Are you praying about God's timing?

Not to mention that I was now chasing after two children.

Once again, there was no turning back. It was a long and slow pregnancy—and more difficult, as the doctor predicted.

In my sixth month, I began having constant contractions. The doctor prescribed higher dosages of drugs, as well as some new ones. Even with the best of care, the outcome was uncertain again.

I was in and out of the hospital in my seventh month as the doctors tried to prolong this pregnancy. Finally, as I stabilized, I was sent home to rest in bed until the baby was due. Phil canceled weeks of concerts and became Mr. Mom. My only outing was to the hospital for stress tests on the baby. There was no guarantee this baby would make it, and it was definitely taking an emotional toll on our family.

Phil was my constant support and help. He learned to run the vacuum cleaner and figured out the dishwasher. Our meals took an interesting turn as Chef Phil laced everything with garlic and cayenne pepper.

The last weeks brought us closer spiritually, and we gained new respect for the role each of us played in our marriage. Phil had a fresh appreciation for what it takes to run a busy household efficiently. For one thing, he had to deal with every mother's frustration of not staying on top of things, not being in control. And I had to let the messes be handled by someone else while I lay flat in bed. That, for me, was harder than it sounds. Our little girls didn't understand why Mommy

After trying to get pregnant for about three years—during which time I had two major abdominal surgeries within the space of eight months—my husband, Randy, and I decided that we had spent enough time in doctors' waiting rooms, undergone enough uncomfortable exams, and suffered through enough rides on the monthly emotional roller coaster. Rather than continue to pursue costly infertility treatments, we slowly released our dream to have a child with my wavy brown hair and Randy's beautiful blue eyes and set our sights on the next logical step—adoption. Ironically, I had never even thought about adoption when I was growing up. I come from a large family and just assumed the ability to get pregnant would be in my genes. Randy, on the other hand, had always thought he would have to adopt as punishment for being mean to his younger adopted brother. Now as we look forward to welcoming a little girl from China into our family in the next year or so, we are both convinced that the opportunity to adopt is not a punishment but rather a beautiful gift from our loving heavenly Father. While we were trying to get pregnant, we made a conscious effort to pray "Nevertheless, not our will, but thine be done" whenever we asked God for a baby. As we wait for our daughter, we know beyond a shadow of a doubt that God heard—and answered—our prayers.

Lois Flowers
Fayetteville, Arkansas

was in bed each day and couldn't be out running around with them. Papa was definitely doing overtime.

I read Philippians 4:13 again and again: "I can do everything through him who gives me strength." This had come to mean to me that Christ is our strength when we are weak—physically, emotionally, and spiritually.

Three weeks before his due date, Ian was born. Phil and I were thrilled to hold a healthy infant son in our arms at last. One day we would tell him about his older brothers. But for now, he seemed content to be cradled in our arms.

I know that our story isn't everyone's story. Not every couple who desires children will be blessed with them. I've found that experiencing the goodness of life has nothing to do with being "good enough," and everything to do with recognizing God's sovereignty. He is eternal and will accomplish—in his way and time—what concerns us.

Is Adoption an Option?

When Phil and I hosted a weekend conference on infertility and adoption, we were amazed to hear how God has blessed and enriched families through the adoption process. Is this God's plan for you? Consider these questions:

1. Are both partners in agreement about the decision to adopt?

2. Is your marriage at a stable point?

3. Are you prepared to take on the financial expenses of an adoption?

4. Are you emotionally and physically recovered from your losses?

5. Are you adopting as a "last resort"? Do you feel adopting is "second best"? If so, you may still have significant unresolved issues that you might find beneficial to address and resolve prior to adopting.

Journal

Journal

Spend My Life with You

by Phil Keaggy

Lay me down to rest,
sing me a sweet lullaby—
when will I see you again?
Sleep come over me.

Can't keep from closing my eyes
The day is gone, but you'll carry on
Watching, protecting me into the dawn
Then another day to spend my life with you.

'Cause there's a hope in my heart
And I believe the day is coming
When we'll never be apart
Just to be where you are
And to spend my life with you
Would be a perfect start.

See you when I rise
Morning will bring me your song
Over and over again
Shine your light on me
Wash me in resplendent love
There is no shame with you as my aim
Yesterday, today, forever the same
And I only want to spend my life with you
In your presence, Lord
There I will be satisfied
Over and over again.[1]

Epilogue

The truths we've learned through years of heartache have proved invaluable. In the midst of pain, we learned strong lessons about life and faith. It was only when Phil and I learned to dig deeply into ourselves and work through painful situations that we discovered what was really important. Pain, whether physical or emotional, takes its toll on our relationships and alienates us from others. If we're not careful, it can close us off from God.

Life is at times painful and sad, at other times it is full of peace and happiness. Doubt and anger can try to crush our trust in God, who offers unfailing love. "Come to me, all you who are weary and burdened, and I will give you rest" (Matthew 11:28), Jesus said. He has the strength to carry us through. When Phil and I cried out in pain and grief, Jesus listened. When we asked why, he understood. When we didn't have the strength to take the next step, he gently pushed us on.

You see, *answers* aren't the real issue. Clinging to God through all of life's circumstances and helping others do the same—that's what's important. Knowing God is what made the difference for us.

Phil and I experienced the loss of our own dreams. We wanted children. We risked our hearts by loving the new lives that grew within me. And when you risk that much—when you risk your own heart—you are most vulnerable to pain. By sharing our personal struggles, we hope we can help women and men whose personal struggles are similar to ours. Who doesn't always want to feel the warm, gracious smile of Providence? But we know it's not always like that. Sometimes you need someone who can help you recognize a deeper shade of grace.

C. S. Lewis said:

> You never know how much you really believe anything until its truth or falsehood becomes a matter of life and death to you. It is easy to say you believe a rope to be strong and sound as long as you are merely using it to cord a box. But suppose you had to hang by that rope over a precipice. Wouldn't you then first discover how much you really trusted it? Only a real risk tests the reality of belief.[1]

Based on what I know, I can tell you this: When you test the rope of God's grace, it will hold you. I promise.

As I look back, I can see that God was acting like a father on his knees at one end of the room, prodding his infant daughter to walk to him. "*You can do it, Bernadette. Come to Papa. I'll catch you! I'm here for you.*" Sometimes we have to stretch our hands so far for help. And God may not pick us up on the first fall, but allow us to get up ourselves and press on.

Why?

Because life is not a black-and-white matter, but full of gray areas. When there are many questions, and the answers are vague or nil, it causes us to stretch a little further to open ourselves to God until we understand that there are deeper shades of grace. As a mother, I soon realized that children were going to teach me new lessons about myself and life.

The focus was no longer on me or on us as a couple, it was on raising children in this world. We were now the responsible parties—and that in itself was pretty scary. In the past, God had used our painful experiences to draw us to him. Now it was this little child and the responsibility of being parents that brought us continually to our knees. Phil spent some sleepless nights struggling with his sense of insufficiency as a father to fully provide for the children God had given us. For me, fear was still an occasional battle.

We now recognized the constant reminders of who really controls the universe and our destiny. Faith is not the belief that God will deliver what we want when we want it, but that he has gracious control of our lives and that he will be faithful to direct our paths and give us the grace to walk through life's unpredictable times.

Lamentations 3:22-23 says: "[God's] compassions never fail. They are new every morning."

Through it all, my hope is that I've become more open and vulnerable to God, and to others in their plight. Life's lessons never end. We can either gain wisdom and understanding from them or let them beat us down. I choose to learn and grow through life's circumstances—and it's a daily choice.

Mercy and grace enough for each day—that is what we are promised. And it is enough.

Journal

Journal

The Answer

BY PHIL KEAGGY

...with this feeling of love in my heart,
my Lord is with me always
And though I know this is just a start,
there are no more dark hallways.
In praise and cheer we're gathered here
with many or with few.
I saw the light, and now tonight
you can see it too.
The answer—you don't need to be alone anymore.
The answer—is Jesus, believe me, he'll open the door...

Resources

Here are just a few of the resources that are available to you if you have experienced miscarriage or the loss of a child. Some of these resource centers are specifically Christian; others are more general.

Support Groups

AMEND
Aiding Mothers and Fathers Experiencing Neonatal Death

4324 Berrywick Terrace
St. Louis, MO 63128
(314) 487-7582
www.amendgroup.org

Bethany Christian Services (adoption)
901 Eastern Avenue NE
P.O. Box 294
Grand Rapids, MI 49501-0294
(616) 224-7610

(616) 224-7550
or 1-800-986-4484
www.bethany.org

CLIMB
Center for Loss in Multiple Births, Inc.
P.O. Box 91377
Anchorage, AK 99509
(907) 222-5321

The Compassionate Friends
P.O. Box 3696
Oak Brook, IL 60522-3696
(630) 990-0010

Hannah's Prayer
Internet-based Christian infertility and pregnancy/infant loss support
P.O. Box 5016
Auburn, CA 95604-5016
e-mail: hannahs@hannah.org
www.hannah.org

March of Dimes Resource Center
Parents or other family members who have experienced the loss of a baby between conception and the first month of life can receive a free kit by calling the March of Dimes Resource Center at 888-MODIMES.
www.modimes.org

M.E.N.D.
Mommies Enduring Neonatal Death
P.O. Box 1007
Coppell, TX 75019

1-888-695-MEND
e-mail: rebekah@mend.org
www.mend.org

MISS
Mothers in Sympathy and Support
P.O. Box 5333
Peoria, AZ 85385
www.misschildren.org

National SIDS Resource Center
(703) 821-8955

Perinatal Loss
2116 NE 18th Avenue
Portland, OR 97212
(503) 284-7426

Pregnancy and Infant Loss Center
1421 East Wayzata Boulevard
Wayzata, MN 55391
(612) 473-9372
www.pilc.org

Resolve
1310 Broadway
Somerville, MA 02114-1779
(617) 623-0744
e-mail: info@resolve.org
www.resolve.org

Dr. Stefan Semchyshyn
Author: *How to Prevent Miscarriage and Other Crises
of Pregnancy*

Holston Professional Building
146 West Park Drive, 9B-1
Kingsport, TN 37660
(423) 224-3600
e-mail: DRSEM@aol.com

SHARE Pregnancy and Infant Loss, Inc.
St. Joseph's Health Center
300 First Capital Drive
St. Charles, MO 63301
(800) 821-6819

SIDS
Sudden Infant Death Syndrome
(800) 221-7437

Stepping Stones
A Christian support group for couples facing fertility challenges or pregnancy loss, and a ministry of Bethany Christian Services.

901 Eastern Avenue NE, P.O. Box 294
Grand Rapids, MI 49501-0294
(616) 224-7488
Fax: (616) 224-7593
e-mail: step@bethany.org

Other Resources

Empty Cradle (information and bimonthly newsletter)
11793 Lake Grove Court
San Diego, CA 92131
(619) 692-2144

Grief Recovery Helpline
1-800-445-4808

(Monday through Friday, 9 A.M. to 5 P.M. Pacific Standard Time)

Internet Resources

www.babyloss.com

www.aplacetoremember.com (good links)

www.sands.org.au (Australian support site)

www.babybunny.net

www.momsonline.com/pregnant/hybri

www.angels4ever.com

http://angiealexander.tripod.com/eastwin

http://members.aol.com/catr101/stand.htm

www.honoredbabies.org

www.homestead.com/wehope

www.modimes.org/healthlibrary2factsheets/miscarriage.htm

www.babycenter.com/refcap/4006.html

www.crha-health.ab.ca/hlthconn/items/miscarr.htm

http://web/ukonline.co.uk/members/ruth.livingstone/little/miscarri.htm#causes (a British site with some general information)

www.gentlebirth.org/archives/miscrgst.html

http://geocities.com/threadsofhope

www.pinelandpress.com/toc.html

www.bbf.org.au (Australian support site)

www.ivf.com

Books

Deborah L. Davis, *Empty Cradle, Broken Heart: Surviving the Death of Your Baby* (Golden, CO: Fulcrum Publishing, 1996).

Sherokee Ilse, *Empty Arms: Coping with Miscarriage, Stillbirth, and Infant Death* (Maple Plain, MN: Wintergreen, 1980).

C. S. Lewis, *A Grief Observed* (San Francisco, CA: HarperSanFrancisco, 2001).

Larry G. Peppers and Ronald J. Knapp, *How to Go on Living After the Death of a Baby* (Atlanta, GA: Peachtree Publishers, 1985).

Maureen Rank, *Free to Grieve* (Minneapolis, MN: Bethany House, 1985).

Mildred Tengbom, *Grief for a Season* (Minneapolis, MN: Bethany House, 1989).

Sheldon Vanauken, *A Severe Mercy* (San Francisco, CA: HarperSanFrancisco, 1987).

Philip Yancey, *Disappointment with God* (Grand Rapids, MI: Zondervan, 1997).

Notes

Chapter One—The Valley of the Shadow

1. C. S. Lewis, "As the Ruin Falls," in *Poems* (New York: Harcourt, Brace, Jovanovich, 1964).

Chapter Two—How It All Began

1. "Happy Are we" by Phil Keaggy © 1993 by Word Music/Sebastian Music. Used by permission.

2. C. S. Lewis, "As the Ruin Falls," in *Poems* (New York: Harcourt, Brace, Jovanovich, 1964).

3. Oswald Chambers, *My Utmost for His Highest* (Uhrichsville, OH: Barbour Publishing, 1998).

Chapter Three—Losing Again

1. National Center for Health Statistics, "Trends in Pregnancy Rates for the United States", 1976-97. NVSR 49(4).

2. Stephanie J. Ventura, et al., "Trends in Pregnancies and Pregnancy Rates by Outcome: Estimates for the United States, 1976-96." National Center for Health Resource Statistics at www.cdc.gov/nchs/data/series/sr_21/sr_21_56.pdf.

3. Joani Nelson Horchler and Robin Rice Morris, "The SIDS Survival Guide: Information and Comfort for Grieving Family and Friends and Professionals Who Seek to Help Them." SIDS Educational Services, Hyattsville, MD, 1994.

4. John DeFrain, et al., *Stillborn: The Invisible Death* (Lanham, MD: Lexington Books, 1986).

5. Ibid.

6. "Growing Up in Heaven" By Nancy Honeytree Miller © 2000 by OakTable Publishing, Inc. Used by permission.

Chapter Four—Dashed Hopes

1. "Carry Your Sorrow No Longer" by Elinor Madeira © 1993 by Little Dude Music. Used by permission.

Chapter Five—Good Grief: Coming to Grips with Loss

1. Ingrid Kohn, et al., *A Silent Sorrow: Pregnancy Loss; Guidance and Support for You and Your Family* (New York: Routledge, 2000).

2. C. S. Lewis, *The Four Loves* (San Diego: Harcourt Brace and Company, 1991).

3. Ibid.

4. Elisabeth Kübler-Ross, *On Death and Dying* (New York: Scribner, 1997).

5. "Michael's Song" by Becki and Scott Hedrick. Used by permission.

Chapter Six—Coping With Well-Intentioned Family and Friends

1. "Disappointment" by Phil Keaggy. Words based on the poem by Edith Lillian Young © 1976 by Birdwing Music and BMG Songs. Used by permission.

Chapter Seven—Marriage and Loss

1. Therese Rando, ed., *Parental Loss of a Child* (Champaign, IL: Research Press, 1986).
2. Sheldon Vanauken, *A Severe Mercy* (San Francisco: HarperSanFrancisco, 1987).
3. Ibid.
4. Ibid.
5. Lynn Friedman, with Irene Daria, *A Woman Doctor's Guide to Miscarriage* (New York: Hyperion, 1996).
6. "One Heart One Life" by Jerry and Sandi Rectenwald © 1995 by Jerry Rectenwald. Used by permission.

Chapter Eight—A Special Note for Husbands

1. Lynn Friedman, with Irene Daria, *A Woman Doctor's Guide to Miscarriage* (New York: Hyperion, 1996).
2. "All Our Wishes" by Phil Keaggy © 1993 by Word Music/Sebastian Music. Used by permission.

Chapter Nine—Finding Grace

1. "Spend My Life With You" by Phil Keaggy © 1980 by Birdwing Music and BMG Songs, Inc. Used by permission.

Epilogue

1. C. S. Lewis, *A Grief Observed* (San Francisco: HarperSanFrancisco, 2001).

Other Good
Harvest House Reading

When Life Is Changed Forever
By Rick Taylor

An honest journey into the depths of God's love for all those who have experienced the complicated and often conflicting emotions brought about by the death of someone near. *When Life Is Changed Forever* offers the sure hope that life can be lived fully again while facing the truth that it can never be the same. Within the pages of this useful book, the author will help you make choices that will better enable you to experience God's "promise of life" even in the midst of your sorrow.

Letter to a Grieving Heart
By Billy Sprague

When a loved one dies, their absence can make going on feel impossible for those left behind. In *Letter to a Grieving Heart*, Billy Sprague offers the kind of compassion and insight that can only come from one who has lived through deep loss himself. With honesty, passion, and perspective, he shares the little things that eased him forward and the words of comfort that carried him to a place of strength. His sensitive and encouraging book will be a welcome companion to see readers through times of grief and heartache.